Businesses Struggling in the Digital Age

Governing Businesses in the Age of Acceleration

Rodrigo Larenas T.

ISBN (Paperback): 9781724195340

2018 EnV - I

For my wife, Paula, and our children

José, Trinidad, Florencia, Rodrigo, and Sofía.

Table of Contents

I. INTRODUCTION 9
II. DISLOCATED BY TECNOLOGY 31
    The inevitable 40
    The digital transformation playbook 42
    The digital vortex 44
    Your strategy needs a strategy 49
    Surviving disruptive technologies................................... 53
    Machines, platforms, and multitudes 55
    Ambidextrous businesses 56
    Some keywords of the Digital Age................................. 57
III. BUSINESS GOVERNANCE IN THE DIGITAL AGE 65
    The challenge of the age of acceleration....................... 66
    Important elements to consider at Level 2 75
        Generate Value 80
        Change the measurement of success 80
        Put the focus on people.. 81
        Harness the power of data 81
        Develop collaborator networks 81
    Important elements to consider at Level 1 84
IV. BLIND TO WHAT IS OBVIOUS AND KNOWN.... 121
V. FINAL WORDS... 165
VI. ACKNOWLEDGEMENTS.. 169

A Zen Story
A Cup of Tea

A Zen master welcomed a university professor
who came to learn about Zen.

The master served tea.
He filled the professor's cup
and he continued pouring more tea.

The professor observed the cup overflowing
until it could contain no more.
"It's too full. No more tea will fit in the cup!"

"Just like this cup," said the master,
"you, sir, are full of your own opinions and paradigms.
How can I teach you about Zen if you do not first empty
your glass?"

I.   INTRODUCTION

> The greatest obstacle to discovery
> is not ignorance - it is the illusion of knowledge.
> Daniel J. Boorstin

> Knowledge is simply a kind of fuel;
> it needs the motor of understanding
> to convert it into power.
> John Wyndham

The Inca Empire was a South American state that covered the largest territory in the history of the pre-Columbian Americas, which came to have around 12 million inhabitants. This territory was called *Tahuantinsuyo* – from the Quechua *tawantin suyu*: the four regions or divisions – and at its peak, it was known as Incanato and/or Incario. It flourished at the height of Incan civilization, in the Andean zone of the subcontinent during the 15th and the 16th centuries. It encompassed around 2 million square kilometers between the Pacific Ocean and the Amazon rainforest, from the outskirts of Pasto (in Columbia) in the north to the Maule River (in Chile) to the south.[1]

Around 1532, *Atahualpa* ascended to the throne of the powerful Inca Empire by executing his older brother *Huáscar* in a civil war there that was precipitated by the death from Smallpox of their father *Huayna Cápac* in 1525. Huayna Capac had not designated successor, and Atahualpa, had crowned himself as the Inca in the city of Cuzco.

In 1532, the Spanish conquistador Francisco Pizarro landed on the South American coast and established a settlement in the north of Peru.

---

[1] https://es.wikipedia.org/wiki/Imperio_incaico

Atahualpa, who was accompanied by between 8,000 and 30,000 men (the number of men varies depending on the source of information), did not consider Pizarro and his mere 168 soldiers a threat, which turned out to be a fatal error.

The meeting place was the city of Cajamarca, which is located some 2,700 meters above sea level and whose name means "town of thorns" in Quechua. On Saturday, November 16, 1532, Pizarro managed to capture *Atahualpa*. He later spared *Atahualpa's* life in exchange for gold, which he then used to defeat the entire Inca Empire.

Months later, when *Atahualpa* had already fulfilled the delivery of gold and silver in exchange for his freedom, Pizarro executed him on July 26, 1533.

As UCLA professor Jared Diamond describes[2]:

> "... The novelty of horses, steel weapons, and guns undoubtedly paralyzed the Incas at Cajamarca...".

In short, even if it is true that there were multiple factors that contributed to the fall of the Inca Empire, such as the disgruntlement of conquered peoples, civil war, and illness, it can be said that the Inca was guilty of trusting too much. Atahualpa's confidence was inflated because he had just won an internal war, that he had a vast empire and that he had significant resources on which to rely.

From a certain perspective, it would seem that Pizarro had in a way, dazzled the leaders of the powerful and admirable Inca Empire. Pizarro managed to *dislocate* the numerical superiority that the Incas held over the Spanish, allowing the latter to take victory with an ease that even they did not expect.

---

[2] Diamond, Jared. *Guns, Germs, and Steel*: The Fates of Human Societies. Norton 1999, p75.

But that fact is not surprising, and it could have been prevented. Human beings act from a limited basis of knowledge, and moreover, we are strongly influenced by our emotions. Because of that, we are subject to cognitive limitations. Herbert Simon (1916 – 2001), Nobel Prize winner in Economics in 1978, proposed that the rationality of the human mind is limited.[3] In very simple terms, he suggested that we human beings are *partially rational*, that we act based on emotional impulses and that our rationality is essentially limited by three factors:

- The information available
- The cognitive limitation of each individual mind
- The time available to make the decision

Then, Daniel Kahneman, a doctor of psychology who received the Nobel Prize in Economics in 2002 along with Vernon Smith, proposed a model of limited rationality to overcome the limitations of people who are supposedly perfectly rational, indicating that the brain basically operates in two systems, which will be explained in Chapter IV.

Even though we will discuss topics related to management and, what's more, to business administration in the age of acceleration, I ask readers to imagine the impact that this must have had on the rulers of the Inca Empire – that is, the result of such a misguided risk assessment of Pizarro's arrival, accompanied by just a few men – and how our rationality and forms of administration could lead us to commit a similar error.

With this last point in mind, I urge you to consider that, as relates to business administration, the board of directors must be prepared to not only "detect" opportunities and threats that have not been evident, but also to manage the organization's timely adaptation and reaction at the speed necessary in the digital age.

---

[3] Herbert A. Simon. Models of a Man. The MIT Press. (You may also see Administrative Behavior, a study of decision-making processes in administrative organizations. The Free Press 1997).

From Atahualpa to the 21st Century

Nowadays, there are many forms of technology in development, and their combination is already producing and will continue to produce opportunities, as well as threats. Some of these technologies will not only leave traditional systems of administration and business management dazzled but also dislocated.

Think of the advances created by Artificial Intelligence (AI), the Internet of Things (IoT), augmented reality (AR), virtual reality (VR), big data, digitalization, the Cloud, electromobility, automatization, robotization, blockchain, quantum computing, nanotechnology, biotechnology, and computer security, just to name a few.

Do you feel comfortable evaluating the risk and potential that these recently names technologies offer to your business? In March of 2015, Tom Goodwin[4] said something that I believe gives a good idea of the impact that new technologies may have on businesses in the digital age: "Uber, the world's largest taxi company, owns no vehicles. Facebook, the world's most popular media owner, creates no content. Alibaba, the most valuable retailer, has no inventory. And Airbnb, the world's largest accommodation provider, owns no real estate."

We are living in a more uncertain, changing business setting than ever before, due to a confluence of factors among which globalization, financial interconnection, a high rate of technological change, and the Internet stand out.

According to an article of HBR titled "The Future and How to Survive It,"[5] the usefulness of large corporations is beginning a long decline, in which they will slide from the almost 10% of the worldwide GDP that they currently represent to 7.9%. The authors indicate, among other things, that the climate is becoming less favorable for businesses in

---

[4] Goodwin, Tom (Mar 3, 2015). "The Battle Is For The Customer Interface." Taken from https://techcrunch.com/2015/03/03/in-the-age-of-disintermediation-the-battle-is-all-for-the-customer-interface/.

[5] Richard Dobbs, Tim Koller, and Sree Ramaswamy (October 2015). "The Future and How to Survive It".

North America and Western Europe due to the entrance of new rivals coming from emerging economies and the tech sector.

They add that these new rivals play by new rules, and that they incorporate the agility and the aggression that many Western businesses lack. Finally, they suggest that, in order to maintain the lead, a company should:

a) Be paranoid,
b) Find "patient capital,"
c) Overcome inertia,
d) Build new intellectual attitudes, and
e) Go to war in search of talent.

Nothing suggests that successful ventures cannot be repeated, such as that of Whatsapp, a business that took an important source of revenue from the great and powerful telecommunications businesses, or that of Uber, whose success was achieved at the cost of reducing the earnings of taxi companies.

Given that, if businesses that have traditionally been stable, such as taxis and telecommunications, could not anticipate their respective threats nor manage to neutralize them, what stops us from seeing new failures as heartrending as those suffered by companies as renowned as Kodak, Polaroid, BlackBerry, Blockbuster or Nokia?

Thus, even in the 21st century, we could have dazzled businesses navigating according to past directions into the "vortex" of failure, while continuing to compensate – in some cases generously – those who will be their gravediggers, instead of adeptly reacting and adapting their organizations to new opportunities. Among the factors that augment the risk of failure for businesses that have been successful, it is important to highlight the following:

- We are living in a digital age and an age of acceleration, a product of multiple, enormous forces, among which stands out the technological advance that has come about as a consequence of "Moore's Law." But what not everyone

understands is that what truly drives the digital transformation is not only technology, but also the interaction between strategy and technology.
- There is risk for executives and board members of successful companies that, dazzled by past successes and operating with a very conservative attitude, maintain business models and approve strategies that have no way of assuring neither the success nor – in some cases – the survival of their companies in the future.
- There are companies in which decisions are made more on instinct that on a solid basis of information. These must be careful not to fall victim to the harms that may be created by the "Hippo"[6] effect, an English acronym that refers to the "highest paid person's opinion."

Moving on, it is necessary to remember that the BCG (Boston Consulting Group) developed a graphic method of analysis for a business portfolio consisting of a matrix with only four quadrants in the early seventies. It relates good market participation (on the horizontal axis) with growth (on the vertical axis) and it is known as the BCG matrix. In this matrix, a product that shows a high level of growth and high market participation is called a "star product." Similarly, a business that shows elevated market participation but a low level of growth is called a milk cow, and it must serve to generate the cash necessary *to create new stars*.

From milk cow to assassin cow

According to Kodak's annual report in 2000,[7] during the year of 1999 around 80 billion photographs were taken, and some 70,000 cameras

---

[6] Marr, Bernard (Oct. 26, 2017). "Data-Driven Decision Making: Beware of The HIPPO Effect!". Taken from
https://www.forbes.com/sites/bernardmarr/2017/10/26/data-driven-decision-making-beware-of-the-hippo-effect/#46d8a9f580f9

[7] Kodak Annual Report Year (2000). p29. https://bib.kuleuven.be/files/ebib/jaarverslagen/KODAK_2000.pdf

were sold. As time has passed, it is estimated that in the year 2014, around 1.5 billion photos were shared each day worldwide through Facebook, WhatsApp, and Snapchat; 90,000 traditional cameras were sold, while around two billion tablets and cell phones with digital cameras were sold. Of the 1.2 billion digital cameras that are believed to have been sold from 1999 to 2014, it is estimated that one billion belong to Google Android users. Moreover, according to the *Statista* website,[8] it is estimated that something like 2.5 billion images could be shared every day across the world in 2018.

The interesting thing is that, in the early 90s, photography was dominated worldwide by giants that would fail, such as Polaroid and Kodak, the latter the inventor of the digital camera in 1975. Other companies also played an important role, such as Canon and Nikon, who, even if they did react and join the digital world, found themselves obliged to share what could have been their slice of the pie[9] with those who played no role: I am referring to iPhones and Galaxys from iOS and Android, respectively.

Beyond valid explanations based in theories linked to innovation,[10] like the one brilliantly proposed by Harvard Business School professor Clayton M. Christensen,[11] there remains a feeling of frustration with the effectiveness observed by board members of the companies in question, which begs questions such as the following:

- What stopped the companies mentioned from using prestige and the significant resources at their disposal in order to become relevant actors in the market of "photographic" cell phones that are currently used?

---

[8] Taken from http://www.statista.com/topics/1164/social-networks/
[9] Spencer, Johnson (September 8, 1998). "Who Moved my Cheese". G. P. Putnam´s Sons. United States.
[10] Taken from http://www.reportr.net/2012/01/19/what-kodak-teaches-us-about-disruptive-innovation/
[11] Clayton M., Christensen and Michael, Raynor (2003). "The Innovator´s Solution". Harvard Business School Publishing Corporation. (For those who would like to learn more about disruptive innovation).

- What operations dynamics did executives use that kept them from maneuvering into a position that would not only ensure their continuity, but rather also assure their leadership in the world of photography?
- Why was Kodak unable to take leadership in digital technology and make it profitable, despite having Steven Sasson, who created the digital camera in 1975, among their ranks, and despite having enormous sums of money available for innovation?
- Why did Kodak not take advantage of the numerous assets that were not threatened by technological change (like their credibility and availability among consumers, the optics that they created, their capacity to manufacture metal frames, their deep knowledge of chemical processes, and more) to develop an effective, strategical response?
- Why did Kodak not use its enormous financial and technological capacities to develop businesses adjacent to their core business and ensure their survival?

Dazzled **businesses with the capacity for** *dislocated* **reaction**

But Kodak is not an exception. There are other businesses that have also fallen victim to important government difficulties in the digital age.

The age of acceleration is demonstrably very challenging for companies' boards of directors, since this age not only makes it more difficult to incorporate new technologies with the demands of the market and business models, but it also allows the borders of industry silos to be broken. This facilitates the appearance of competitors from unexpected places (or industries). It allows the appearance of undetectable competitors.

An interesting example to consider is that of WhatsApp. WhatsApp's business model launched a direct "attack" on the heart of a technological industry that not only did not know how to anticipate nor detect the threat, but also took so long to react that the attacker's advantage was used by a company in a different industry.

WhatsApp, founded in 2009 by Brian Acton and Jan Koum, two former Yahoo! employees, began offering a free messaging service that competed with the text messages (SMS) that telephone companies offered. It then added voice messages, and later also added video chat. It has not ceased to amaze me that the service developed by WhatsApp was not developed from within one of the biggest telephone companies in the world, and that once detected, it was not acquired by any of them.

WhatsApp, with only 55 employees and 417 million users, was bought by Facebook on February 19, 2014, for $19 billion (USD). Not by Telefónica, not by China Mobile, not by Deutsche Telekom, nor by any other telecommunications giant. According to the business intelligence company OVUM,[12] OTT (over-the-top) services offered by companies such as WhatsApp and Skype, among others, will cost the telecommunications industry at large, from 2012 to 2018, something like $386 billion (USD).

The idea of opening this book with these brief reflections on the giants in their respective industries, widely recognized around the world, is not to perform autopsies on them. On the contrary, the reflections only intend to serve as shocking examples to propose the following to all who are responsible for business operations and government:

- If a company with the resources, innovative capacity, and positioning that Kodak had failed to ensure its continuity and to restructure the business, what makes you think that your company – one that probably has less talent, recognition, and resources – is not at risk of being *dazzled* by its past and allowing its capacity for reaction to be *dislocated* by poor assessment, suffering a deadly fate as well?

---

[12] http://fortune.com/2014/06/23/telecom-companies-count-386-billion-in-lost-revenue-to-skype-whatsapp-others/

- If an entire industry, such as telecommunications, that had the technological understanding, capital, and multinational presence did not know how to react in time to a threat that it could not detect and that, once detected, did not know how to evaluate correctly, what makes you think that your company, *dazzled* by past results, is not at risk of repeating such an error of detection and reaction of the same sort, *dislocating* its ability to react?

Considerations to adapt to the digital age

In the 19th century, industry experienced the introduction of steam engines, which created enormous mechanical force that was then relayed through factories by means of conveyor belts and axles. The impact that this technology had on productivity was so great that, according to Erik Brynjolfsson and Andrew McAfee of MIT, the steam engine is the invention that has had the greatest impact in the history of humanity.[13]

Corporate inertia

However, when electric technology was able to replace steam-powered machines, the change took longer than expected.

Stanford University economist and professor emeritus Paul A. David[14] confirms that the use of electricity for industrial applications took between 30 and 40 years to produce the potential productivity increases that the technological advantage offered. This is because, though companies replaced steam engines with electric motors, they

---

[13] Brynjolfsson, Erik y McAfee, Andrew (2014). "The Second Machine Age: Work, Progress, and Prosperity in a Time of Brilliant Technologies". W.W. Norton & Company. Page 6, position 136.

[14] David, Paul A, 1990. "The Dynamo and the Computer: An Historical Perspective on the Modern Productivity Paradox," American Economic Review, American Economic Association, vol. 80(2), pages 355-361, May.

did so while keeping the plant locations and designs[15] for steam engines. That is, the generation of employees trained in the era of steam power had to stop working so that the new generation could change the workflow and then make use of electric machines, according to the new capabilities that they offered.

As will be discussed in the next chapter, today there are several technologies advancing at an incredible speed. There is no doubt that the advances, combined with new customer demands, will create new business opportunities, which will also threaten to destroy organizations that are not prepared to adopt new technologies and to adapt their organizations and business models in time. It should be remembered that, as early as 1942, Joseph A. Shumpeter stated that "creative destruction" was an element essential for capitalism[16].

It is important to understand that, prior to the digital revolution, technology played a secondary role for many companies. In fact, it was seen as more of a facilitator for existing processes than as a tool capable of driving current business and creating new businesses. But we are apparently repeating the mistake made in the shift from steam to electricity. An article published by McKinsey in July of 2018, entitled, " Memo to the CFO: Get in front of digital finance – or get left back,"[17] proposes that companies are just now experiencing the first stages of the application of digital technologies to finance processes in forms that are capable of generating higher efficiency, more knowledge, and long-term value as well. In fact, if you look at the current state of things, you can see that it is not uncommon for the ERP of companies to be largely oriented to accomplishing tasks associated with accounting, depending on the Chief Financial Officer (CFO), the

---

[15] Brynjolfsson, Erik y McAfee, Andrew (2014) "The Second Machine Age: Work, Progress, and Prosperity in a Time of Brilliant Technologies". W.W. Norton & Company. p102, position 1513.

[16] Schumpeter, Joseph A. (1994) [1942]. Capitalism, Socialism and Democracy. London: Routledge. pp. 82–83. ISBN 978-0-415-10762-4.

[17] Chandra, Kapil; Plaschke, Frank and Seth, Ishaan (July 2018). "Memo to the CFO: Get in front of digital finance – or get left back". Taken from https://www.mckinsey.com/business-functions/strategy-and-corporate-finance/our-insights/memo-to-the-cfo-get-in-front-of-digital-finance-or-get-left-back?cid=soc-web

executive who is paid to limit the risks taken by the company, not to experiment or innovate.

If "modern" companies do not want to repeat the delay suffered by companies that used steam engines while incorporating electric motors – using them under the same conditions as steam engines for almost forty years – they must take measures at least to understand a) what technology offers, b) what the market demands, and c) what abilities – in terms of the equipment as well as of knowledge and people – must be incorporated.

New forces in action

In his book "Thank You for Being Late,"[18] Thomas L. Friedman suggests that we are living in the era of acceleration, characterized by the existence of three enormous forces:

i. Moore's Law and the consequences it has had for technology
ii. Mother Nature, with the effects of extreme climates that are seen in various parts of the world, and
iii. Market, or said in another way, the effects of globalization

As I understand it, beyond being disruptive, the combination of these three forces has the capacity to produce a true "dislocation" of the ability of companies to respond, leaving them vulnerable to damaged prestige or even a deadly fate.

Digital leaders take the reins

If you look at the list of the five largest companies on the U.S. stock exchange[19] from 2001 to 2016 (a summary is shown in the table

---

[18] Friedman, Thomas L. (November 22, 2016). "Thank You for Being Late: An Optimist's Guide to Thriving in the Age of Accelerations". Farrar Straus & Giroux.

[19] Desjardins, Jeff (August 12, 2016). "Chart: The Largest Companies by Market Cap Over 15 Years." Taken from http://www.visualcapitalist.com/chart-largest-companies-market-cap-15-years/

below), you can see that, with the exception of Microsoft (which is otherwise a tech company) the top-ranked companies in 2001 no longer appear on the list in 2016, and, on the contrary, companies that were small or did not exist in 2001, such as Facebook, had joined it.

On June 26, 2018, after 111 years in business and after losing 80% of its value since 2000,[20] GE General Electric was removed from the "Dow Jones industrial average."

Largest Companies traded on the Stock Exchange

Año	N° 1	N° 2	N° 3	N° 4	N° 5
2001	G&E 406 B U$D	MicroSoft 365 B U$D	Exxon 272 B U$D	Citi 261 B U$D	Walmart 260 B U$D
2006	Exxon 446 B U$D	G&E 383 B U$D	Total 327 B U$D	MicroSoft 293 B U$D	Citi 273 B U$D
2011	Exxon 406 B U$D	Apple 376 B U$D	PetroChina 277 B U$D	Shell 237 B U$D	ICBC 228 B U$D
2016	Apple 582 B U$D	Alphabet 556 B U$D	MicroSoft 452 B U$D	Amazon 364 B U$D	Facebook 359 B U$D

Similarly, on August 2, 2018, Apple became the first company to reach a market capitalization of $1 billion (USD), and it is followed by Amazon, with $895 million (USD); Alphabet, with $858 million (USD); Microsoft, with $826 million (USD); Facebook, with $509 million (USD); and Alibaba, with $473 million (USD).

In addition to this, Yale professor Richard Foster[21] has argued that the average lifespan of a company belonging to S&P 500 has shrunk from 67 years in 1920 to today's estimate of only 15 years.

---

[20] Oyedele, Akin (Jun 20, 2018). "GE is getting booted from the Dow Jones industrial average; Here are the members of the original 1896 index." Taken from http://www.businessinsider.com/dow-original-companies-2016-12

Change in competitive advantages

The digital age has made making prototypes cheaper and simpler by, for one example, using 3D printers. This reduces the comparative advantages that existed between companies that traditionally dominated the market and entrepreneurial potential.

Columbia University Professor Rita Gunther McGrath states the following in her book *The End of Competitive Advantages*:[22]

> Chances are the strategies that worked well for you even a few years ago no longer deliver the results you need. Dramatic changes in business have unearthed a major gap between traditional approaches to strategy and the way the real world works now.
>
> In short, strategy is stuck. Most leaders are using frameworks that were designed for a different era of business and based on a single dominant idea—that the purpose of strategy is to achieve a sustainable competitive advantage. Once the premise on which all strategies were built, this idea is increasingly irrelevant.

In addition to the above, IBM carried out a study in which they interviewed more than 5,000 business leaders from more than 70 countries and 20 different industries, and they discovered what they called "horizontal innovation"[23]. This can be summarized by saying that it was easier to anticipate where competition would come from in the

---

[21] https://www.theatlantic.com/business/archive/2015/04/where-do-firms-go-when-they-die/390249/
[22] https://www.ritamcgrath.com/books/the-end-of-competitive-advantage/
[23] http://www.onlydeadfish.co.uk/only_dead_fish/2016/06/horizontal-innovation.html

past, and that nowadays, there is a greater risk of competition staying invisible – until it is too late.

Failures on the board of directors

An article published in the Harvard Business Review[24] in early 2015 dramatically stated that boards of directors were not working, indicating, for instance, the fact that only 16% of the 772 board members interviewed by McKinsey in 2013 said that their boards had a deep understanding of the industry in which they worked.

A badly-run board of directors can, in turn, become part of and victim to a host of other problems, such as:

a) The inability to react: As in the case of Kodak, the board of directors that governed the company did not effectively react to a threat identified in the eighties. Perhaps they were dazzled by good results from the "film" unit.
b) The inability to anticipate and detect: As in the case of WhatsApp, those who govern telecommunications companies did not anticipate, detect, or take advantage of the benefits that OTT services generated, which left space for Facebook to enter the industry. Perhaps they were dazzled by good results from their other business units.
c) Horizontal Innovation: It seems that the traditional formulas used to establish and manage a strategy do not take into account the modern-day difficulty in detecting "invisible" competitors.

Radar for Boards of Directors

If we agree on a) the inertia that companies exhibited to move in time, that is, to adopt changes as needed; b) the new forces coexisting in the

---

[24] Barton, Dominic and Wiseman, Mark (Jan-Feb 2015). "Where Boards Fall Short". Harvard Business Review.

marketplace, as proposed by Thomas L. Friedman; c) the leadership taken by companies that manage to dominate digital technologies; d) the changes to that were traditionally considered competitive advantages; and e) the deficiencies signaled among boards of directors, companies were faced with an atmosphere in which "traditional" references no longer held true, due to the high rate of change, it may then be asked:

- How would it help companies to rely on government agencies that are able to act as needed when traditional systems have been or are at risk of being *dislocated*, that is, being removed from their place or context?
- Is it not necessary to provide boards of directors with a mechanism to detect and monitor, a kind of radar which allows them to detect risks and thus provides them with the essential information to better govern their companies?

Cows can nurture stars

In January 2012, Kodak filed for "Chapter 11,"[25] US bankruptcy law. The ironic thing is that on almost the same date, March 31, 2012, at the close of its fiscal year, Fujifilms reported revenues of almost $27 billion (USD)[26] (2,195 billion yen).

But as early as the 80s, both Kodak and Fujifilm realized that photography would become digital in the future. Both companies continued to make use of traditional photography while investing in digital technologies and diversifying into new areas. At both companies, members of the "traditional movie" units (films) were in control, and at both companies, they took a long time to admit that it was an area of business that would disappear in the future.

---

[25] UNITED STATES COURTS. Chapter 11 – Bankruptcy Basics. Taken from http://www.uscourts.gov/services-forms/bankruptcy/bankruptcy-basics/chapter-11-bankruptcy-basics

[26] Fujifilm annual report 2012. Taken from https://www.fujifilmholdings.com/en/pdf/investors/integrated_report/ff_ar_2012_all

So if the market forecast, strategies, and internal policies were similar, why did the results diverge? According to an article published by *The Economist* in January 2012, the big difference in the fates of Kodak and Fujifilm was execution:[27] "Kodak acted like a stereotypical change-resistant Japanese firm, while Fujifilm acted like a flexible American one."

While approaches that are intended to help will be revealed throughout the book, I just want to preview the following ideas here:

a) It is possible to identify numerous examples of companies that, for various reasons, were affected by the consequences of internal decisions and omissions that were "disconnected" from their immediate realities, rather than by competitive moves, technological change, or the market.

b) It seems that there are shareholders, directors, founding partners, and executives who are unaware that organizations – not unlike living organisms – have life cycles.[28] They grow, develop, and reach maturity, then begin to decline in old age and finally die or, in the case of some companies, are reborn.

c) Likewise, it does not seem evident that a company's competitive advantages are not permanent, but are transitory,[29] so that they are lost as time passes. Nor is it recognized that companies develop inertia that limits their adaptability.

d) The current technological development and the speed at which different technologies advance, obliges the members of the boards not to be dazzled by the successes achieved and to be prepared to review and adapt the strategy of the company hand in hand with the potentials offered by the new technologies.

---

[27] Shumpeter (Jan 18, 2012). "Sharper focus". Taken from https://www.economist.com/schumpeter/2012/01/18/sharper-focus

[28] Pitirim Sorokin, born in Russia, lived from 1889 to 1968. He immigrated to the United States in 1923, and he was a professor at Harvard from 1930 to 1959. There he founded the department of sociology, and he developed important work on the theory of social cycles.

[29] Rita Gunther McGrath. "Transient Advantage". HBR June 2013.

From the traditional point of view, which should not be forgotten, one frustrating aspect is that, beyond the apparent causes for the disappearance of some companies, the failures often did not originate from causes "of the market" but because of causes more accurately located within the company. That is to say, they were victims of what a soccer fan might call an "own goal" or a tennis player an "unforced error".

Looking at the challenges created by technological development, another frustrating aspect is that some failures at renowned companies could have been avoided if a different strategy had been implemented.

Think about Toys "R" Us. Founded in 1948 as a children's furniture factory, it became the toy store that stole our hearts by Charles Lazarus in 1957. After decades of successes, it filed for Chapter 11 bankruptcy in September 2017, after years of declining sales and rising debts. While the intense price war among large retailers such as Walmart, Amazon, and Target contributed to the company's problems, Toys "R" Us did not innovate in its business model, incorporate technology, or adapt to changing consumer behaviors.[30]

Situations that companies such as Kodak have experienced, or how phone companies faced WhatsApp, or Toys "R" Us, impart a lingering feeling that they were *slow by design*. In the book *How Google Works*, Eric Schmidt and Jonathan Rosenberg indicate that many companies are run to minimize risks, not to maximize their freedom and speed.[31] They add that information is packaged more than shared, and that lines of power place decisions in the hands of the few.

---

[30] http://knowledge.wharton.upenn.edu/article/the-demise-of-toys-r-us/#
[31] Neil Perkin and Peter Abraham. Building the Agile Business through digital transformation: how to lead digital transformation in your workplace. April 2017. p32.

In simple terms, as Scott Brinker explains with the so-called Martec Law, change within companies occurs at a slower rate than that at which technology evolves – and that at which consumers adopt new technologies.[32]

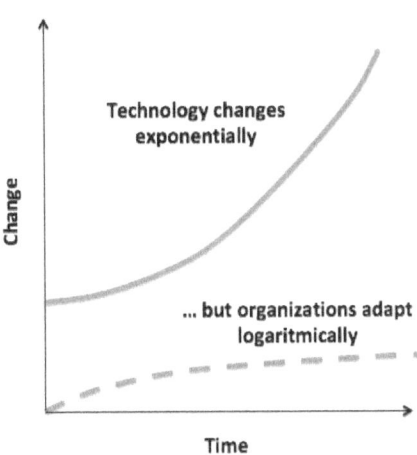

Therefore, this book's approach is that companies must have a board with the capacity, skills, knowledge and dedication necessary to help management face the dynamics of the digital age; to adapt the company and its culture to the changes demanded by the market in a timely way, while converting internal and external threats into opportunities. That is, governing the company well.

The challenge we face is creating the mechanisms needed so that human adaptability and, in this case, that of companies, can react according to the speed of technological change. It is, then, crucial that boards of directors are composed of competent individuals, as is

---

[32] https://chiefmartec.com/2016/11/martecs-law-great-management-challenge-21st-century/

maintaining an adequate work dynamic, which I will call a "vigilant attitude."

It is important to make it clear that I am not suggesting that it is appropriate to double a company's administration. The idea is that, in light of the market's continuous evolution and the acceleration of technological change, it is important to have an experienced group who is knowledgeable about business and who helps the executives in charge of company administration take necessary actions so that the company reaches its *maximum development potential* (MDP).

What can you expect from this book?

This book has been written from a practical perspective, combining visions and models developed by multiple experts, as well as real-world examples, to facilitate the understanding of key points. The information summarized here only aims to show that businessmen, executives, and directors – however successful they have been in the past – are liable to make mistakes and omissions, which can even prove fatal for their organizations.

As you accompany me through this book, I will try to convince you that, in order to avoid being dazzled by the digital age, you not only must adopt the appropriate technologies, but also implement good strategies and appropriate corporate administration practices.

In Chapter II, different ways of facing the challenges of the digital age are summarized as developed by leading thinkers, which I imagine will be useful to asking the right questions for each company.

Chapter III will, in light of the difficulty that current human systems have to adapting to technological change, present a tool that aims to serve as an instrument for directories to improve administration: it is a kind of "radar" for boards of directors, tuned to detect threats and opportunities not detected by the company's management. This idea come as a consequence of the double loop learning theory [33], stablished by Argyris and Schön:

> When the error detected and corrected permits the organization to carry on its present policies or achieve its presents objectives, then that error-and-correction process is single-loop learning. Single-loop learning is like a thermostat that learns when it is too hot or too cold and turns the heat on or off. The thermostat can perform this task because it can receive information (the temperature of the room) and take corrective action. Double-loop learning occurs when error is detected and corrected in ways that involve the modification of an organization's underlying norms, policies and objectives.

In Chapter IV, I will reiterate the premises of basic business governing principles. I will insist that mistakes made by companies stem more from internal decisions or indecisions than from external circumstances, given that adaptation is an internal decision. I will argue that companies often harbor an under-used potential, and that they can therefore improve their operations if they have a well-organized board that focuses on strategy, on trying to understand the dynamics of technological development, and on setting a good work ethic from a somewhat paranoid point of view, what I call a "vigilant attitude."

With all this in mind, I hope that the information revealed throughout the book does not give answers, but instead prepares you to ask the right questions for the success of your respective companies.

I hope the book is of interest to you.

Note 1: The book is intended to help boards of directors that have already reached a certain degree of maturity. That is, those that Adizes

---

[33] http://infed.org/mobi/chris-argyris-theories-of-action-double-loop-learning-and-organizational-learning/

characterizes as being at a stage of plenty or even maturity (Chapter IV); this is not for startups.

Note 2: In addition to radar, I also refer to Dr. Adolfo Gutierrez's opinion: "The reason why large companies cannot react is – in some cases –due to political frictions as well. There, profit centers exert a lot of power, even during decline, and they all underestimate the effect that companies and emerging technologies will have in 10 years. The VCs upset the balance of power. Well-funded startups concentrate a huge amount of resources on the weakest flanks of established companies, so emerging companies rob you of the most profitable markets, which are often emerging, while established companies work to defend all their markets, with almost no regard for projections, the future. The political power of 1,000 employees and their managers is enormous, even if their sales are stagnant. They are the ones who actively block the most visionary teams in companies that, even when small and losing money, can be generating momentum for the next stage.

Note 3: On the question of gender, we mention directors, owners, and managers in a general way throughout the book, with the understanding that these positions may be occupied by women and men.

II.   DISLOCATED BY TECNOLOGY

> We can ignore reality,
> but we cannot ignore the consequences
> of ignoring reality.
> *Ayn Rand*

> That is what learning is.
> You suddenly understand something
> you've understood all your life,
> but in a new way.
> *Doris Lessing*

The conclusion of a study done by MIT Sloan Management Review, in collaboration with Deloitte University Press, "Strategy, not Technology, Drives Digital Transformation," was the following:

> Digitally maturing companies behave differently than their less mature peers do. The difference has less to do with technology and more to do with business fundamentals. Digitally maturing organizations are committed to transformative strategies supported by collaborative cultures that are open to taking risk. Equally important, leaders and employees at digitally maturing organizations have access to the resources they need to develop digital skills and know-how. [34]

---

[34] Kane, Gerald; Palmer, Doug; Philips, Anh; Kiron, David and Buckley, Natasha (Summer 2015). "Strategy, not Technology, Drives Digital Transformation. Becoming a digitally mature enterprise". From
https://www2.deloitte.com/content/dam/Deloitte/es/Documents/tecnologia/Deloitte_ES_Tecnologia-Strategy-not-techonology.pdf

The report, developed after interviewing 4,800 executives from 27 industries and 129 countries, concludes that a business cannot reinvent itself digitally unless it has, on one hand, a) a clear digital strategy that has the support of high-level management, which consists of leaders who promote a culture that can change and can invent new things; and on the other hand, b) the support of the right professionals.

Relevant data of the Digital Age

According to an article published in Forbes [35], it has been estimated that, though something like 16.3 ZB (Zetabytes: 10^{21} bytes) of data was created worldwide in 2017, this number will reach about 163 ZB by the year 2025. That is, it will grow tenfold in only eight years. According to other contributor to Forbes, Bernard Marr, we are producing 2.5 quintillion (2.5 x 10^{18}) bytes of data every day (in 2018) [36]: as a reference, you may like to know that there were 5 Exabyte (5 x 10^{18}) of information created between the dawn of civilization through 2003, but that much of information was created every two days.[37]

Part of this growth is due to the simultaneous "contribution" of several "laws" that I find important to know, and that will be mentioned briefly below:

Moore's Law. On April 19, 1965, Gordon Moore, at that time the research leader of "Fairchaild Semiconductors" and later a co-founder of Intel, said that technology had a future, that the number of transistors per surface unit in integrated circuits would double every

---

[35] Cave, Andrew (Apr 13, 2017). "What Will We Do When The World's Data Hits 163 Zettbytes In 2025?" From https://www.forbes.com/sites/andrewcave/2017/04/13/what-will-we-do-when-the-worlds-data-hits-163-zettabytes-in-2025/#4f8cbfb4349a

[36] https://www.forbes.com/sites/bernardmarr/2018/05/21/how-much-data-do-we-create-every-day-the-mind-blowing-stats-everyone-should-read/#704c6ec960ba

[37] Neil Perkin & Peter Abraham. Business through Digital Transformation (p. 15). Kindle edition.

year, and that the trend would continue for at least the next ten years.[38]

Later, in 1975, he modified his own prediction, stating that the pace would fall, and that the capacity for integration would not double every 12 months but approximately every 24 months. This period is sometimes mistakenly cited as 18 months because of Intel executive David House, who predicted that the performance of the chip would double every 18 months (a combined result of more and faster transistors). This progression of exponential growth, doubling the capacity of integrated circuits every two years, is called Moore's Law.

However, in 2007 Moore himself determined an expiration date: "My law will cease to be fulfilled within 10 or 15 years." He said this during the same conference where he stated that a new technology would nonetheless come to replace current technology.

The direct consequence of Moore's law is that prices will go down as benefits go up. This law currently applies to personal computers and cell phones. However, there were no microprocessors invented when it was formulated in 1971; nor were there personal computers, popularized in the eighties, nor cellular or mobile phone services.

Brian Krzanich, CEO of Intel until June 2018, summarized the impact of the so-called "Moore's Law," explaining that Intel engineers calculated that if a Volkswagen Beetle had evolved as the 1971 processor 4004 did in relation to the Core i5 of 2015, the car would be able to go 300,000 miles per hour (483,000 km/hr), at about 2 million miles per gallon (3.2 million km per 3.8 liters) at a cost of 4 cents.

But Moore's Law also served as an impetus for other noteworthy advances, in what may be called sister technologies; some which are mentioned below.

---

[38] https://es.wikipedia.org/wiki/Ley_de_Moore

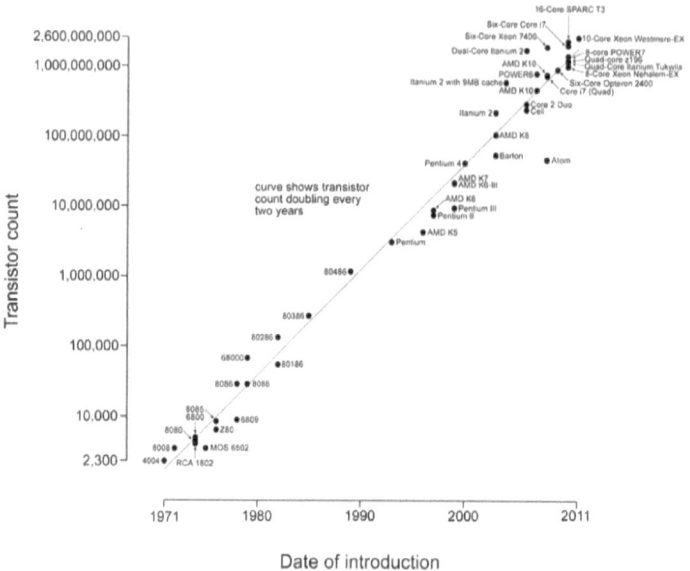

Source: OFFGRID[39]

Koomey's Law states that the energy required for computing is halved every 18 months. This lesser-known trend in (electrical) energy efficiency has been remarkably stable since the 1950s, long before the microprocessor was invented. In fact, it is more "accelerated" than Moore's Law since, according to the Koomey, the number of calculations per kilowatt-hour doubles approximately every 1.57 years, compared to that of Moore which at this time doubles closer to every two years.

---

[39] McCarthy, Patrick (May 2, 2017). "Infographic: the growth of computer processing power. over the last six decades, computing power has skyrocketed, and it's not slowing down yet". From https://www.offgridweb.com/preparation/infographic-the-growth-of-computer-processing-power/#

Kryder's Law is the equivalent of Moore's Law for data storage. It states that the maximum number of bits that will "fit" onto a hard-drive also doubles approximately every 18 months.

In 1980, Seagate introduced the world's first 5.25-inch hard drive (remember floppy disks?), which could store up to 5 MB of data for $1,500. Thirty-five years later, you could buy a 6,000 GB unit from the same company for $600. That represents an increase of one million percent in storage capacity, along with a seven-fold decrease in price (accounting for inflation). Not even silicon chips can boast that kind of progress.

Butters's Law says that the amount of data that "leaves" an optical fiber doubles every nine months, which means that the cost of transmitting a piece of data in an optical network decreases by half in that same amount of time. Unfortunately, that rate of progress does not quite reach consumers: Nielsen's Law establishes that the bandwidth available for the average domestic user only doubles every 21 months. Even so, it is an exponential rate, and it is why telecommunications companies have been able to make so much money while reducing the cost of data traffic.

Cooper's Law is even more remarkable than Moore's Law. The first radio broadcast was made by Marconi in 1895. A century ago, radio technology could only accommodate about 40 separate conversations across the planet. The Law states that the maximum number of voice conversations or equivalent data transactions -that can be conducted in all of the useful radio spectrum over a given area- doubles every 30 months.

As an example, the following table presents a summary of relevant aspects associated with advances in cell phone technology:

Generation	1G	2G	3G	3.5G	4G	5G
Period	1970 - 1980	1990-2000	2001-2004	2004-2005	2011-	>2020
Band With	2 Kbps	64 Kbps	144 Kbps	> 2 Mbps	200 Mbps a 1Gbps	> 1 Gbps
Technology	Celular análogo	Celular digital	GPRS, EDGE, CDMA	EDGE, Wi-Fi	WiMax, LTE, Wi-Fi	

Haitz's Law states that the amount of light generated by LEDs ("light emission diodes") is multiplied by 20 and that the cost per lumen (unit of useful light emitted) decreases by a factor of 10 every decade for a given wavelength of light.

The exponential improvements in LED technology mean that it is becoming the leading way to generate light. Brighter and more efficient lighting is available at a lower cost in homes, while it means that LED lighting can now be used for more specialized commercial applications, such as lighting in large stadiums and amphitheaters. All this translates into lower electricity consumption, as well as generally lower carbon emissions and fewer of the toxins such as mercury used in old lighting. It is not surprising that these types of technologies are improving so rapidly. All of them run on silicon, the basis of semiconductor materials found in computers and communications networks.

Metcalfe's Law Metcalfe's Law was originated by George Gilder, but it is attributed to Robert Metcalfe [40], co-inventor of Ethernet (1980). It refers as much to the growth in the number of connections as to value. Given that the Internet as we now know did not exist when the law was formulated, it refers more to the value of devices in general, such as having one fax machine, which is useless. When there are two fax machines, you can communicate with one other person, but when there are millions the device has some value.

---

[40] https://www.techopedia.com/definition/29066/metcalfes-law

Over time, Metcalfe's Law has been linked to the substantial growth of the Internet and its operation, in line with Moore's Law. The concept is similar to the business concept of a "network effect," given that a network's value provides both additional value and a competitive advantage. For example, eBay may or may not have had the best auction site, but it is clear that it had the majority of users. Because it is so difficult to replicate, the power of the network drives out competition.

Metcalfe's Law is a concept used in computer and telecommunications networks to represent the value of a network. The law states that the impact of a network is the number of nodes in the network squared. For example, if a network has 10 nodes, its inherent value is 100, or 10 × 10. The end nodes can be computers, servers, and/or connected users.

The gap between company growth and technological development

Given the "laws" shown, if the growth rate of transistor density is exponential – as is the growth rate of data storage, LED brightness, and the creation of that data – and that their transmission rate is exponential, yet the growth rate of traditional businesses is linear and furthermore generally moderate, what can be expected to happen with respect to the difference (the gap) between the two growth rates?

It seems clear that there are entrepreneurs of the "digital age" who are interested in and capable of occupying the space that exists between the exponential growth rate of technologies and the moderate growth rate of "traditional" companies. This implies a risk for companies who, dazzled by these successes, are prevented from reacting in time.

The origin of these difficulties

It is difficult for the human mind to comprehend exponential growth, such as those described in Moore's Law, and projecting the impact of this sort of trend is problematic.

Legend has it that[41] a king named Sheram once ruled long ago in a region of India. It is said that, in one of the battles fought by his army, the king lost his son, which left him so deeply troubled that nothing that his subjects offered him could cheer him up.

One day, a certain Sissa came to his court and requested a hearing. The king accepted it and Sissa presented him with a game that he guaranteed would amuse the king and cheer him up again: chess. After explaining the rules and handing him a board and its pieces, the king began to play, and he was amazed: he played and played, and his grief largely disappeared.

King Sheram, grateful for such a precious gift, told Sissa that he could ask for whatever he wanted as a reward. After thinking about it, Sissa asked for one grain of wheat for the first square on the chessboard, two for the second one, four for the third four, eight for the fourth, and so on ...

The king considered the request to be unworthy of his generosity, and he told Sissa, "By asking me for such a meager reward, you underestimate – and irreverently so – my benevolence. As wise as you are, you should have shown more faith before the goodness of your sovereign. You will receive the amount of wheat that corresponds to the 64 squares of the board as you wished: for each box double quantity that for the previous one. You may go. "

But it turns out that it was the king, not Sissa, who had underestimated the amount of wheat promised, since the number actually reached 18,446,744,073,709,551,615 grains.

---

[41] Artacho, Amadeo (March 10, 2014). "La leyenda del tablero de ajedrez y los granos de trigo". From https://matematicascercanas.com/2014/03/10/la-leyenda-del-tablero-de-ajedrez-y-los-granos-de-trigo/

	1	2	3	4	5	6	7	8
1	1	2	4	8	16	32	64	128
2	256	512	1.024	2.048	4.096	8.192	16.384	32.768
3	65.536	131.072	262.144	524.288	1.048.576	2.097.152	4.194.304	8.388.608
4	16.777.216	33.554.432	67.108.864	134.217.728	268.435.456	536.870.912	1.073.741.824	2.147.483.648
5	4.294.967.296	8.589.934.592	17.179.869.184	34.359.738.368	68.719.476.736	137.438.953.472	274.877.906.944	549.755.813.888
6	1,09951E+12	2,19902E+12	4,39805E+12	8,79609E+12	1,75922E+13	3,51844E+13	7,03687E+13	1,40737E+14
7	2,81475E+14	5,6295E+14	1,1259E+15	2,2518E+15	4,5036E+15	9,0072E+15	1,80144E+16	3,60288E+16
8	7,20576E+16	1,44115E+17	2,8823E+17	5,76461E+17	1,15292E+18	2,30584E+18	4,61169E+18	9,22337E+18

$$T64 = 1 + 2 + 4 + 8 + 16 + 32 + \ldots + 9.2 \times 10^{18}$$

$$T64 = 18{,}446{,}744{,}073{,}709{,}551{,}615 \text{ grains}$$

Given that there are approximately 25,000 grains of wheat per kilogram and that the wheat production of the 2013/2014 harvests yielded 708,891,000 tons, it may be said that the amount of grains promised by the king equals 737,869,762,948 tons, the worldwide production of grain over about 1,044 years.

While there are different versions of and conclusions to this story, I would like to warn you that many companies risk misjudging reality as they experience it, as happened to King Sheram. On the one hand, the human brain does not have to speed to solve nonlinear calculations, which leaves us vulnerable to making mistaken judgments, open to the risk of becoming totally "dislocated by the digital age".

Continuing in this line of thought, Moore's law turned 50 in 2015. If we consider that processing speed has on average doubled every two years for more than 50 years, in terms of the chessboard we could say that we are entering what can be called "the second part of the board." That is, a world where the human brain cannot fathom the consequences of the amounts associated with future advances.

In an effort to develop effective corporate administration mechanisms for the current age of "acceleration," a summary of the conclusions published by leading thinkers in the field is presented below.

The inevitable [42]

Kevin Kelly, founder and executive director of the magazine *Wired*, proposes that there are twelve trends that are unavoidable:

"Becoming"	"Cognifying"
"Flowing"	"Screening"
"Accessing"	"Sharing"
"Filtering"	"Remixing"
"Interacting"	"Tracking"
"Questioning"	"Beginning"

"Becoming:" Turning into something else. Moving from set products to services and subscriptions that are always being updated. For Kelly, given the rate of exponential changes that we experience, we have all become novices, regardless of the experience we think we have.

"Cognifying:" Adding knowledge with artificial intelligence. Making everything more intelligent by using powerful artificial intelligence (AI) from the Cloud. For Kelly, there are three factors that have accelerated the development of AI: i) low-cost parallel processing, ii) big data, and iii) better algorithms.

"Flowing:" This refers to constant change. It means that processes are more important than products. We go from a daily mode to real time. We depend on transmissions in real time for everything. Our attention has shifted from possession of "material" goods to the flow of intangible goods. The values are: i) immediacy, ii) personalization, iii) interpretation, iv) authenticity, v) accessibility, vi) embodiment, vii) sponsorship, and viii) the ability to make discoveries.

---

[42] Kevin, Kelly (2017). "The Inevitable: Understanding the 12 Technological Forces That Will Shape Our Future." Penguin Books.

"Screening:" Living on screens. Converting every surface into a screen. People of this age prefer multitasking, parallel processing, reading texts in a non-linear fashion, and having images instead of words.

"Accessing:" Changing from a society where we have assets to one where we will instead have access to services at all times. Access becomes more important than ownership since, in an ever-changing, ever-updating world, ownership ceases to carry the meaning it once did. There are five identifiable trends that will accelerate the transition from having to accessing: i) dematerialization, ii) demand in real time, iii) decentralization, iv) synergistic platforms, and v) the cloud.

"Sharing:" Large-scale collaborations are preferable. The economy of sharing also includes sharing property. For Kelly, everything that can be shared will be faster, cheaper, and come in forms that are as of yet unknown to us.

"Filtering:" Taking advantage of highly-detailed personalization to anticipate our desires. In a world where information is abundant, that which is scarce; thus, where our attention flows, there the money will flow.

"Remixing:" Mixing again. Breaking down existing products into their most primitive parts and then recombining them in every possible way. The idea is that innovation comes out of prototype development based on existing technologies that, when combined, allow new technologies to emerge.

"Interacting:" Diving into our computers to maximize their ability to support us and getting all our devices to interact. For Kelly, the future of new technologies depends on the ability to discover new interactions in which there will be both augmented reality and virtual reality.

"Tracking:" Using the ability to monitor everything possible to benefit citizens and consumers. This includes not only geographical position, but also considerations linked to diet, health, rest, etc. For Kelly, surveillance will be as inevitable as it is ubiquitous.

"Questioning:" Fostering good questions is much more valuable than getting good answers. Kelly believes that new inventions create new gaps in knowledge that must be discovered with good questions.

"Beginning:" Kelly believes that the inevitable marks the beginning of something greater that we do not now see. A new way of thinking will be created; there will be new progress, and with this, there will also be new harms to be assuaged.

The digital transformation playbook [43]

Digital transformation has the potential to be disruptive, and in so many different ways. David Rogers, a professor at Columbia University and author of the book *The Digital Transformation Playbook*, discusses five arenas – arenas that must be used by companies to be successful – in which technology is acting and changing the rules: data, innovation, competition, value, and customers.

Data Data is now ubiquitous in a world of social networks and mobile technologies. There are large amounts of data – enormous, in fact – that are available to the consumer's benefit; however, these are also available to companies that wish to use them to improve the products and services they offer.

Innovation This is a process through which companies develop new ideas, test them, and put them on the market. In a world of digital economy, we are seeing that rapid tests can be done with innovation in ways never seen before. This is accelerating the cycle of innovation, and it is allowing companies to conduct real-time experiments with their products and execute prototypes in a very affordable way.

Competition One of the ideas of digital transformation is that it often facilitates the entry of other players into an industry. We should

---

[43] David L. Rogers (2016). *The Digital Transformation Playbook*. Columbia Business School Publishing.

therefore expect an increase in competition in all the fields impacted by digital transformation. This is because digital technology seems to be eliminating the (traditional) boundaries that exist between different industries, and companies that were once partners may increasingly become rivals. For example, think of how Google, Apple, and Amazon compete more and more in several arenas within the field of digital technology.

Value Nowadays, we can see new ways of offering value in very creative ways, taking advantage of digital technology. With Uber, for example, digital technology is used to offer a new value proposition in an industry that has not experienced any changes for decades.

Clients Clients are evolving. The ubiquity of information allows customers to be very well-informed, and this facilitates a reduction in loyalty as compared to the past. For example, a customer today may check out a product in a physical store, then buy it from another company on the internet.

What all this means is that, in the end, the old sources of competitive advantage are disappearing. Things like natural monopolies, which are shaped by scarce resources, are, though still important, at risk. In Rogers's increasingly common view, strategic assets will no longer be owned by the company, but companies will have access to them through networks of suppliers.

The great challenge of the digital age is, then, converting data – those large amounts of data that you have within companies – into useful information. On the other hand, and unlike in the past, digital technologies allow the simple and affordable development of tests, prototypes, and experiments.

Rogers states that, according to his research, there are five conducts that facilitate client adoption of digital technologies, which he calls "behaviors characteristic of clients in the network:"

- Access digital data, content, and interactions in the fastest, easiest, and most flexible way possible

- Get involved with digital content that is sensory, interactive, and relevant to your needs
- Customize the experiences by choosing and modifying a wide variety of information, products, and services.
- Connect to share experiences, ideas, and opinions through texts, images, and social networks
- Collaborate by working together, as we are social animals.

David Rogers also points out the convenience of creating business platforms not just to offer products. By platforms, we mean a business that creates value by facilitating transactions between two or more types of clients. [44]

The digital vortex [45]

The International Institute for Management Development (IMD) in Switzerland has, together with Cisco, developed the Global Center for Digital Business Transformation.

The DBT has developed the comparison with a vortex to indicate how every industry where businesses operate risks suffering the disruptive impact of digitalization, even those that believe that they might not be subject to such forces.

DBT has established that digital business models can be grouped into three categories:

---

[44] David L. Rogers (2016). *The Digital Transformation Playbook*. Columbia Business School Publishing. P. 56, position 1105.

[45] Loucks, Jeff; Macualay, James; Noronha, Andy; and Wade, Michael. (2016). "Digital Vortex. How Today's Market Leaders Can Beat Disruptive Competitors at Their Own Game." International Institute for Management Development. From http://digitalvortex.imd.org/wp-content/uploads/2016/06/Digital-Vortex-Excerpt.pdf

Cost Value

Cost value refers to the area in which the competitive effects of digital disruption are likely to be more noticeable because the competitor reduces the prices offered to the end customer. A remarkable and memorable example of this category is the Amazon Kindle, which can reduce costs to customers through product "dematerialization."

Relevant aspects of this model are:

- Low prices or free
- Price transparency
- Prices based on the consumer
- Reverse auctions
- Distribution of costs, reimbursements and rewards

Cost value is also created when a company (a disrupter) moves from nudging its way into an industry to being an established provider. For example, in the travel industry, there are websites that people use to book hotel accommodations and car rentals, and to purchase airfare, which exerts pressure on or caps prices that these services can charge.

Experience Value

Experience value is generated by offering (to customers) products or services that are more convenient, given, for example, context or level of control, which does not imply that they are cheapest. A memorable example in this category is that of Netflix, a company that offers a digital service that allows customers to "unpackage" services offered by cable TV companies.

Relevant aspects of this model are:

- Empowering the customer
- Personalizing service
- Automating tasks
- Making things easier for customers

- Allowing any device to be used at any time

Platform Value

The eigenvalue of a platform is unique to the digital age, and it offers what is called network externality (Metcalfe's Law) [46], situations in which the increase in the number of users increases the value that is created. A good example is that of Facebook, a network that generates value when many people use it.

Relevant aspects of this model are:

- Creating ecosystems, such as the Apple iOS
- "Crowdsourcing," such as WikiLeaks
- Communities, such as Twitter
- Digital community, such as Airbnb
- Data orchestration, such as SAP

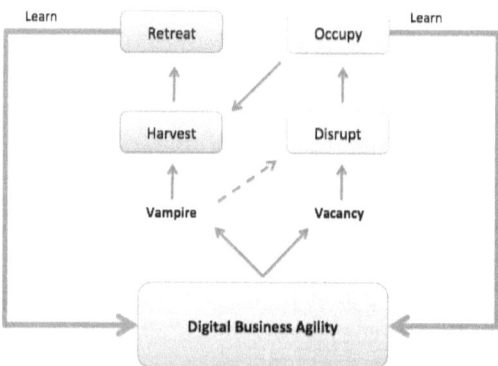

The DBT has also identified two realities emerging from the seizure generated by digital disruption:

---

[46] https://es.wikipedia.org/wiki/Ley_de_Metcalfe

a) Value vampires
b) Value vacancies

The so-called *value vampires* refer to a type of disruptive company in the digital era that is characterized by creating serious problems for the rest of the companies on the market: they are "dangerous." They are essentially an extreme type of company whose competitive advantage completely "drains" the income and/or profits of companies that operated in a certain market.

The so-called *value vacancies* refer to another type of company in the digital era that is characterized by taking advantage of market opportunities that can be profitably exploited through the use of digital technologies and their business models: they are "good" disruptive companies.

According to the DBT, although there is no recipe that can face this technological disruption that guarantees success, companies must develop a certain capacity that is "agility in digital business."

The DBT's experience indicates that one of the most formidable enemies for an established company – as large and prestigious as it may be – can be a small enterprise. The latter can use digital technologies combined with a business model capable of providing a new mix of cost value, experience value, and platform value.

Defenses in the digital era

As the DBT indicates [47], "the speed of technological change, the innovation of business models, and the mix of industries accelerate as companies are absorbed by the digital vortex."

---

[47] Bradley, Joseph; Loucks, Jeff; Macaulay; Noronha, Andy; Wade, Michael (November 2015). "Disruptor and Disrupted." Global Center for Digital Business Transformation an IMD and Cisco Initiative. p2.

Therefore, given the complexities of the digital age, the best defense companies can develop is one of digital agility.

Digital agility means an organization's ability to use digital media to change, which rests on three pillars: hyperawareness, informed decision-making, and rapid execution.

Hyperawareness refers to the ability that companies must develop to detect and monitor changes that occur in the environment where they develop their businesses. It provides the "lifeblood" of the two pillars that sustain the agility of digital business: informed decision-making and rapid execution.

Informed decision-making allows data to be analyzed and distributed in order to support strategic decisions. This depends on the quantity and quality of data obtained through hyperawareness.

Rapid execution should guide the efforts and direction of the entire company.

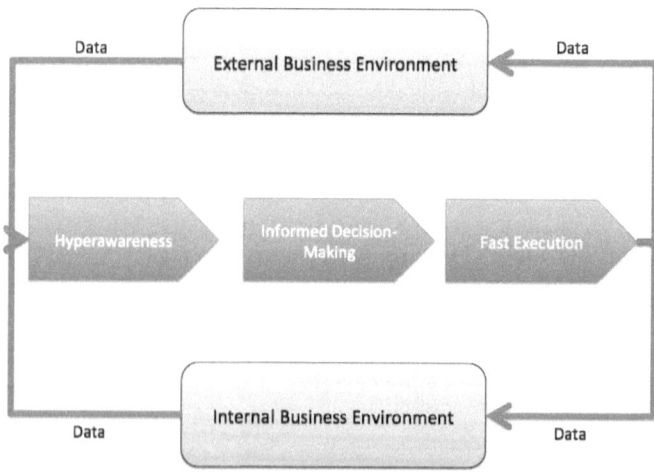

Your strategy needs a strategy [48]

The authors of the book *Your Strategy needs a Strategy* state that a company must consider the very different scenarios at play to be successful in today's world, and those scenarios in turn make it necessary to use strategies adapted to each of the five environments identified, as mentioned below:

- Classic
- Adaptive
- Visionary
- Self-adjusting
- Renovation

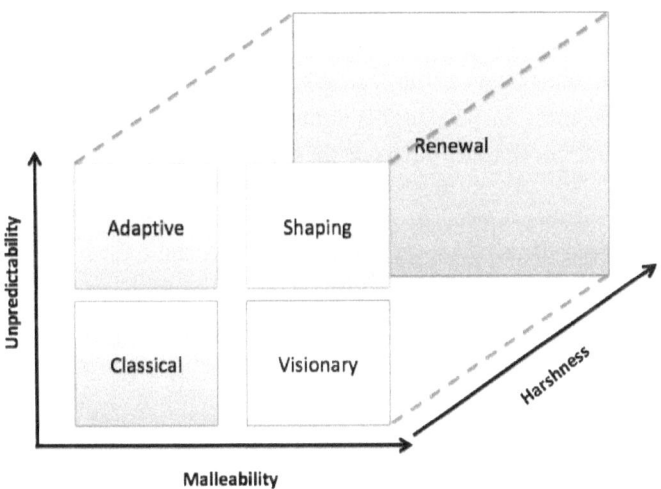

---

[48] Reeves, Martin; Haanes, Knut; Sinha, Janmejaya (2015). "Your Strategy needs a Strategy. How to Choose and Execute the Right Approach." Harvard Business Review Press.

Classic 🖉 Be Great

In a classic environment, it is possible to predict or anticipate the demand of a market that is not very malleable with certainty. In this environment, there are strong brand names and few technological changes, and this allows deep analyses from which to draw a basis of information for detailed planning, which must then be well-executed.

The companies in this environment operate in a way that could be called sequential. This is due to the fact that they carry out an exhaustive analysis followed by detailed planning in the first stage. In the second stage, they concentrate their efforts on executing and controlling excellent performance.

Adaptive 🖉 Be Fast

In the adaptive environment, changes come quickly and do not permit planning as would a classic environment: you cannot plan, but you can experiment, select, and climb. An adaptive strategy should be used when the business environment is difficult to predict and, at the same time, difficult to adapt. You have to experiment, select, climb, and adapt.

As an example of this strategy, the authors cite the Inditex company Zara, which introduced this approach in two ways in 1975: a) shortening the supply chain by bringing manufacturing closer to customers, and b) generating "smaller" production lots in order to react to market preferences for the season.

Visionary 🖉 Be the First

Something that does not exist is created. It comes from the entrepreneur who creates, adapts, and envisions something new or revolutionary. This approach is characterized by three stages.

i. Forecast an opportunity, taking advantage of the beginnings of a mega-trend, using a new technology, or offering a dormant demand or dissatisfaction.

ii. Be the first to form a company that offers the product or service.

iii. Persist in meeting objectives while maintaining flexibility to overcome unforeseen difficulties.

Timing is critical in this approach since it allows one to define market standards, influence customer preferences, etc. But if the process comes too early, there is a risk that potential customers will not be ready for the product; if it is late, the company will be seen as an imitator.

As an example of this strategy, the authors cite UPS, a company that in 1994 recognized that electronic commerce would create a change in the industry, invested large sums of money in IT, and positioned itself as the best system for electronic commerce deliveries, by making tracking online purchases easy.

Adjustment 🖉 Be the orchestrator

Ecosystems that are influencing and generating mutual adaptations. The adjustment strategy is appropriate when there is an opportunity to rewrite industry standards for an industry that has just started, one that is very dynamic, that has been disrupted, or that is fragmented. This is because it allows stimulating demand, developing the infrastructure required, and minimizing regulatory barriers that may exist or arise.

As an example, the authors cite the strategy followed by both Google and Apple when they transferred "app" development for Android and iOS, respectively, to third parties. This invitation to external developers was beneficial for both parties, at a time when market leader Nokia released the platform Symbian, which did not offer flexibility suitable for developers.

Renewal 🖉 Be Viable

Very complex conditions in which the company is just trying to survive. The focus of activity is on freeing up resources.

The idea of the model at hand is not to label the company but the different lines of products or services, since different realities coexist in the same company, particularly if it operates in multiple markets. Given this, they suggest that the "collage" of proposed strategies be vibrant and dynamic over time.

The authors raise the importance that the company itself "self-interrupts" its business, not a competitor. To achieve this, they suggest balancing the allocation of resources between the *use* of current resources and the *exploration* of new possibilities, for which they suggest three techniques:

- Exchanging people between exploration and use units
- Creating separate units for exploration and use
- Creating an ecosystem, complementing the exploration and use units with not only internal but external resources as, well

In either case, an important part of success is linked to the permanent adjustment of resources assigned to one. For example, you can start by assigning 10% of resources to exploration and 90% to use; proportions may vary depending on the circumstances to ensure a proper balance between both (what is called *ambidexterity*), which will depend on the business environment and its evolution.

Surviving disruptive technologies

Henry C. Lucas, professor at the University of Maryland, argues that disruptive technology may be understood as an innovation that offers a product or service that is so convenient that target customers quickly abandons the traditional way of doing things and turns to the new. [49]

The participants in this contest could be summarized as the following actors:

The innovative company:

- Inventor (s)
- Implementers

The titular company:

- Board members
- CEO
- Employees

For purposes of this book, it is very important to understand that board members have an important role to play.

In the "traditional" world – prior to the digital age – a company could enjoy a period of "stability" in which there were few changes once it reached a certain level of success. Then, they would detect small changes and react with a few adjustments, thereby regaining control of the business.

In the digital age, in which we are already living, discontinuities are more frequent, and changes are stronger.

Incumbents are faced with the following dilemmas:

---

[49] Lucas, H. C. (2012). "En búsqueda de la sobrevivencia. Lecciones de las Tecnologías Disruptivas." From https://cicm.org.mx/wp-content/files_mf/20171106.pdf

- Denial
- History
- Resistance to change
- Change of mentality
- Brand
- Sunk costs
- Cost effectiveness
- Lack of imagination

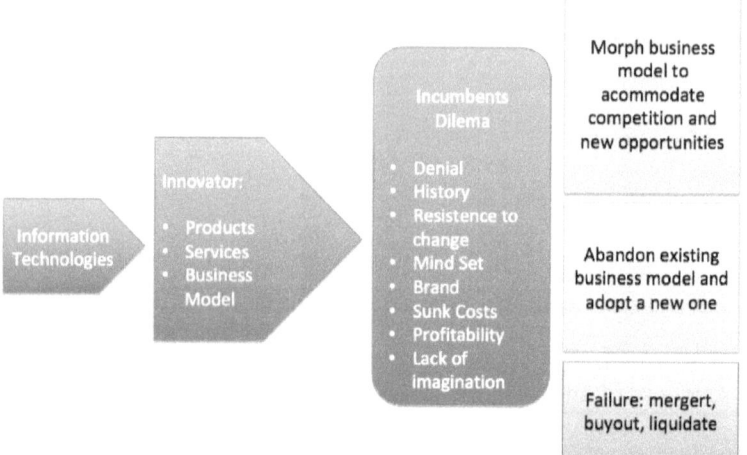

According to Lucas, the possible results facing attacks from competition with new information technologies may be summarized as follows:

- Adapting the business model to be ready for new opportunities
- Abandoning the current business model and adopting a new one
- Failing and finding one-self obligated to sell, merge, etc.

Machines, platforms, and multitudes [50]

MIT professors McAfee and Brynjolfsson state that there are three major trends in the era in which we live that we must learn to balance:

a) Trend 1: the rapid increase in the capacity of the machines, exemplified by the advances made in artificial intelligence, such as the triumph of a machine over a player of the complex strategy game called "go." The counterpart of machine intelligence (AI) is the human mind.

b) Trend 2: The appearance of young, large companies with significant power to influence markets by establishing platforms, such as Airbnb, Uber, or Facebook. The counterparts of these platforms are products and services that have traditionally been the source of income for companies.

c) Trend 3: The emergence of the use of crowds as support for the development of new products and services. Recognizing that, no matter how good a company's team is, they cannot replace the knowledge and experience of the entire market. The counterpart of crowds is the heart of the business, meant to be its knowledge, experience, processes, etc.

The authors emphatically insist that it is not about the human mind, the products and services, or the heart of the business becoming obsolete or outdated. On the contrary, they still consider these to be essential for business's success.

Therefore, given the strides made by technology, the essential thing is for companies to rethink the balances between the following with fresh eyes:

- Machines and the human mind
- Platforms and products and services
- Crowds and the heart of the business

---

[50] McAfee, Andrew and Brynjolfsson, Erik (2017). "Machine, Platform and Crowd, Harnessing our digital future." W.W. Norton & Company.

Even when the balance between exploration and use is highly relevant, companies tend to favor use over exploration because of the risk of not generating income fast enough, as needed for investment in the latter.

UC professor and Stanford PhD Michael Leatherbee defines ambidexterity as follows:

> "Ambidexterity (which comes from the ability to use the right or left hand indistinctly) is the ability of organizations - rare and difficult to develop - to efficiently provide current products or services (exploit), while developing others that could be provided in the future (explore). The result of ambidextrous ability is the opposite of the saying "bread for today and hunger for tomorrow".

The tendency to favor use may create what is called a *competition trap* in which the company would be efficient but less so, as it continues to improve current processes instead of seeking a superior one.

Now, when an organization focuses more on exploration than use, it is possible that it will find new ideas on which it cannot turn a profit. This is called the *experimentation trap*.

Companies that find the right balance between exploration and use are called ambidextrous.

Considering this, I would like to summarize the highlights of the study conducted by Enrique Canessa [51], professor at the UAI, working with other researchers:

a) He highlights three main results of his research:

---

[51] Canessa-Terrazas, Enrique; Morales-Flores, Javier; Maldifassi-Pohlhammer, José (2017). "The impact of IT-enhanced organizational learning on performance: evidence from Chile." Revista Facultad de Ingeniería, Universidad de Antioquía. From http://www.scielo.org.co/scielo.php?pid=S0120-62302017000100060&script=sci_abstract&tlng=en.

- The use of information technologies (IT) to improve existing practices (use) allows a company to improve short-term results.
- In contrast to the previous point, when companies make use of information technology (IT) for exploration, they tend to adjust their processes and structures to newly acquired knowledge.
- There seems to be a tendency to favor use over exploration, which can be even more damaging for companies that operate in emerging markets and are subject to greater volatility.

b) He concludes that companies that excessively favor use over exploration will not be well prepared to face "upsets" in the market. Companies that operate in emerging markets therefore should take robust measures to avoid falling prey to competition.

Some keywords of the Digital Age

Artificial Intelligence (AI)

AI is a branch of computer science that studies computer models capable of performing human activities based on two of its primary characteristics: reasoning and behavior.

The advances achieved by the AI are truly amazing, and it seems appropriate to highlight two examples related to games:

- Chess: In 1996, the IBM supercomputer named Deep Blue – and later Deeper Blue in 1997 – managed to dethrone chess champion Gary Kasparov. [52]
- Go: This Asian game is approximately 3,000 years old, and it is characterized by being much more complex than chess. In

---

[52] https://es.wikipedia.org/wiki/Deep_Blue

2016, Google program AlphaGo defeated go world champion Lee Sedol, and it did so by teaching itself to learn.

Just to give an idea of the complexity of the game, a researcher[53] calculated that a chessboard has something like 4.3 × 1019 possible combinations, while go has an astonishing 2 × 10170 possible moves. This explains the 20-year difference it took for AI to win the chess and go championships, while also highlighting the advances made in AI.

The term "artificial intelligence" was formally coined in 1956 during a Dartmouth conference, but by then, it had been in the works for five years. During that time, many different definitions had been proposed that were not fully accepted by the research community.

In 1956, John McCarthy coined the term "artificial intelligence," defining it as "the science and engineering of making intelligent machines, especially intelligent computer programs."[54]

For Nils John Nilsson,[55] there are four basic pillars on which artificial intelligence rests:

- The search for the necessary state in the set of states produced by the possible actions
- Genetic algorithms (analogous to the evolutionary process of DNA strands)
- Artificial neural networks (analogous to the physical functioning of human and animal brains)
- Reasoning through formal logic (analogous to abstract human thought)

MIT professors Erik Bryonjolfsson and Andrew McAfee[56] suggest that the first machine revolution was essentially manufacturing

---

[53] ALVY (9 Mar 2015). "Un investigador calcula el número de posiciones posibles para el juego de Go (versión simplificada)". Economía Digital. From https://www.microsiervos.com/archivo/ordenadores/calculo-posiciones-posibles-go.html

[54] Cosein (Oct. 29, 2016). "Inteligencia artificial." From http://www.cosein.com/2016/10/29/inteligencia-artificial/

mechanisms capable of increasing available force beyond human force, always requiring people to make decisions. In what is now called the second age of machines, cognitive tasks are being automated to the level that artificial intelligence can, in some cases, make even better decisions than human beings.

The Internet of Things (IoT)

The Internet of Things is a concept that refers to the digital interconnection of everyday objects with the Internet. It was proposed by Kevin Ashton at MIT's Auto-ID Center in 1999, where research was conducted in the field of radio frequency identification (RFID) and sensor technologies.

According to the Gartner Company, in 2020 [57] there will be approximately 26 billion devices worldwide connected to the Internet of Things. On the other hand, Abi Research ensures that there will be 30 billion wireless devices connected to the Internet by that same year [58]. With the next generation of internet applications (IPv6 protocol) all those objects could be identified, something that could not have been done with IPv4. This new system would be able to instantly identify any type of object by means of a code.

It is estimated that the number of devices connected to the internet will increase at a rate of 30% per year until 2025.

---

[55] Club de Innovación. "Todo lo que deberías saber sobre Inteligencia artificial". From http://www.clubdeinnovacion.com/bloginn/-que-es-inteligencia-artificial

[56] Brynjolfsson, Erik and McAfee, Andrew (January 25, 2016). "The Second Machine Age: Work, Progress, and Prosperity in a Time of Brilliant Technologies." W.W. Norton & Company.

[57] Gartner (December 12, 2013). "Gartner Says the Internet of Things Installed Base Will Grow to 26 Billion Units By 2020." From https://www.gartner.com/newsroom/id/2636073

[58] Tecnología al Instante (02/02/2017). "IoT = Internet of Things (Internet de las Cosas)". From https://www.abiresearch.com/press/more-than-30-billion-devices-will-wirelessly-conn

Augmented Reality

This term is used to define seeing a physical environment in the real world through a technological device. This device (or set of devices) adds virtual information to the existing physical information; that is, it adds a synthetic, virtual part to reality. In this way, tangible physical elements are combined with virtual elements, thus creating augmented reality in real time.

Augmented reality is different from virtual reality; the former overlays a visual reality generated by technology onto the material reality of the physical world, and the user perceives a mixture of the two realities. In contrast, with virtual reality, the user is isolated from the material reality of the physical world and is immersed in a totally virtual scenario or environment.

Big Data

Also known as macro-data, massive data, data intelligence, or large-scale data, Big Data is a concept that refers to large data sets so large that traditional computer applications of data processing cannot deal with them.

This is a set of data or combinations of data sets whose size (volume), complexity (variability), and rate of growth (speed) make it difficult to capture, manage, process, or analyze them using conventional tools and technologies, such as relational databases and conventional statistics or visualization packages, fast enough to be useful [59].

Although the standard size of a given data set considered Big Data is not firmly defined and continues to change over time, most analysts and practitioners currently refer to data sets ranging from 30-50 Terabytes to several Petabytes as Big Data.

---

[59] https://www.powerdata.es/big-data

The complexity of Big Data is primarily due to the unstructured nature of much of the data generated by modern technologies, such as web logs, radio frequency identification (RFID), sensors in devices, machinery, vehicles, internet searches, social networks like Facebook, laptops, smart phones and other mobile phones, GPS devices, and call center records.

In order to effectively use Big Data, it must in most cases be combined with structured data (usually from a relational database) from a more conventional commercial application, such as an ERP (Enterprise Resource Planning) or a CRM (Customer Relationship Management).

Computation in the Cloud

The concept of "cloud computing" is very broad and covers almost all possible types of online services. When companies offer a service hosted in the cloud, they usually refer to one of these three modalities: Software as a Service (SaaS), Platform as a Service (PaaS), and Infrastructure as a Service (IaaS).

Cloud computing consists of servers, which are responsible via the internet for meeting requirements around the clock. You can access information or services through an internet connection from any mobile device or landline worldwide. They serve users from various common providers around the world, thus allowing lower costs and guaranteeing greater availability.

"Cloud computing" is a new model for offering business and technology services. It gives users access to a catalog of standardized services and allows them to respond to their business needs in a flexible and adaptive manner, in case of unforeseeable requests or spikes in work. They only pay for what they use, or even receive service free of charge from suppliers financed through advertising or non-profit organizations.

The changes that cloud computing offers are an increase in the number of services based in the network. This creates benefits both for suppliers, who can offer a greater number of services more quickly and efficiently, and for users who can access them, enjoying the "transparency" and immediacy of the system and the pay-what-you-use model. Likewise, the consumer saves salary costs or the costs of economic investment (premises, specialized material, etc.).

Finally, cloud computing can also reduce CAPEX and the TCO (total cost of ownership), and it facilitates upward mobility.

Automation

Industrial automation (automation: from ancient Greek *auto*, "guided by oneself") refers to the use of computerized and electromechanical systems or elements for industrial purposes.

As an engineering discipline – one broader than a control system – automation encompasses industrial instrumentation, which includes sensors, field transmitters, control and supervision systems, data transmission and collection systems, and real-time software applications to supervise and control plant or industrial process operations.

Blockchain

Block-chain is a data structure in which information is grouped in sets, or blocks, to which meta-information is added relative to a previous block in the chain in a timeline, so that, thanks to cryptographic techniques, the information contained in a block can only be rejected or edited by modifying all subsequent blocks. This characteristic allows it to be applied to a distributed environment, so that the blockchain data structure can act as a non-relational public database that contains an irrefutable historical record of information [60].

---

[60] Investopedia. From https://www.investopedia.com/terms/b/blockchain.asp

In practice, block-chain has, thanks to asymmetric cryptography and hash functions, allowed the implementation of a distributed ledger, supporting and guaranteeing the security of digital money.

Cybersecurity

The question is not whether a cyber-attack will occur, but rather when we will fall victim to an attack.

Computer security, also known as cyber-security or information technology security, is the field related to computer science and telematics that focuses on protecting computer infrastructure and everything related to it; this especially includes the information stored in a computer or circulating through computer networks. To this end, there are a series of standards, protocols, methods, rules, tools, and laws designed to minimize possible risks to infrastructure and information.

Cybersecurity includes software (databases, metadata, files), hardware, computer networks, and everything of value to the organization that may pose a risk if this confidential information falls into the hands of other people, becoming, for example, privileged information.

III.   BUSINESS GOVERNANCE IN THE DIGITAL AGE

> Just because nobody complains
> doesn't mean all parachutes are perfect.
> *Benny Hill*

> It is not because things are difficult that we do not dare.
> It is because we do not dare that they are difficult.
> *Seneca*

Chilling precedents

At the beginning of 2015, an article published in the Harvard Business Review caught my attention.[61] It gave some information about improper operations that were observed by some boards of directors and that had been collected from surveys conducted by McKinsey in 2013 and 2014, along with the Canada Pension Plan Investment Board (CPPIB):

- Only 34% of the 772 directors surveyed in 2013 recognized that the boards on which they served had a deep understanding of their companies.
- Only 22% said that their boards understood in depth the way in which their companies created value.
- Only 16% said that their boards had strong knowledge of the dynamics of the industry in which the company operated.
- Of the 604 executives surveyed in 2014, when asked about who was responsible for the excessive focus on the short term and the low emphasis on the long term, 47% indicated that it was the boards.

---

[61] Barton, Dominic and Wiseman, Mark (JANUARY-FEBRUARY 2015). "Where Boards Fall Short". Harvard Business Review.

In short, the article reveals a highly inconvenient situation for business management: many of the directors surveyed recognized that the entities (boards) where they served did not have a deep understanding of their companies' strategies, the way in which they create value, or the dynamics of the industry in which they operate.

The challenge of the age of acceleration

Thomas L. Friedman and Eric A. Teller argue that human beings and the organizations that we have created have a limited ability to take on or adapt to change, which has been growing at a linear rate. Technological development, on the other hand, experiences an exponential rate of change, which has nowadays exceeded the rate of change of human beings. [62]

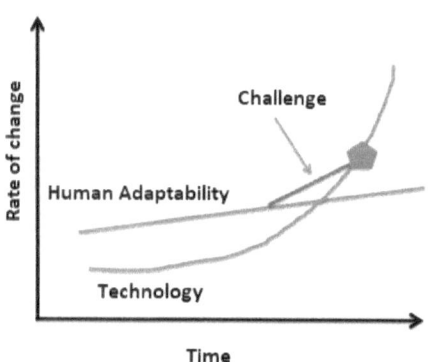

---

[62] Taibbi, Matt (NOVEMBER 28, 2016). "The Official Thomas Friedman 'Make a Meaningless Graph Contest". From
https://www.rollingstone.com/politics/features/official-thomas-friedman-make-a-meaningless-graph-contest-w452465

Today we see companies whose business models have been *disrupted* by the changes resulting from the use of new technologies. These are companies whose governance has ended up being *dislocated* by this acceleration, bringing about not only the loss of the ability to anticipate threats, but also the ability to react and adapt to the new reality in order to take advantage of the opportunities.

Perhaps the boards produced habits of governance that were valid in a period of sustained and relatively stable growth, such as that observed in industrialized countries after World War II. But it is a simple fact: if there was ever a period of linear growth when plans were based on predictable demand, it seems to have ended.

Facing the challenge

For the success of a company to be sustainable in the age of acceleration driven by digital technologies, having governance abilities superior to those that existed "before" is necessary.

Boards of directors cannot let themselves be *dazzled* by the digital age with the excuse that they are not of this era, protecting themselves by contemplating the dairy cows – of which they are proud – in the rearview mirror. They cannot afford to repeat the mistakes that led to the *dislocation* of the reaction times of once powerful companies such as Kodak, Polaroid, Nokia, Toys "R" Us, and many others.

While administrative actions will still be implemented by a general manager and their executive staff; in the digital age, the board cannot become an entity dedicated to be "contemplating" the results presented by administration. On the contrary, board members must have an active role in company governance; they will hopefully develop an "almost paranoid fear" of not taking necessary actions so that the company can evade its next threat and take advantage of what will be its next opportunity, all in time.

The challenge is then to create mechanisms that allow boards to improve their sensitivity, to learn faster, in order to finally manage governing quickly and effectively based on relevant information.

Aerial analogy: observe, orient, decide, and act

Organizations and companies across the world face a crisis of agility. Confronted with an unpredictable dynamic external environment, they are forced to adapt at a speed for which they simply have not been designed and, therefore, for which they are not prepared.

History tells us that, during the Korean War, an American pilot named John R. Boyd challenged his teammates that, starting from a disadvantaged position, he could be in a good position in their aircraft lineup in 40 seconds, or he would them pay $40.

The story's accuracy aside, what's certain is that "40-Second Boyd" developed a technique that could explain why American pilots flying F-86 aircraft achieved better results at a 10:1 ratio over North Korean pilots, flying MiG-15s, in circumstances where the latter airships were considered superior.

Boyd called his method "OODA," meaning observe, orient, decide, and act.

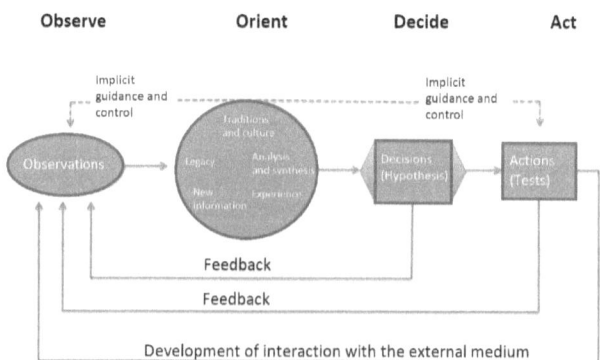

In applying his method, he discovered that the American F-86s had only two small advantages over the Mig-15s: they had better visibility, and they could change combat tactics more quickly because they had hydraulic controls.

By implementing Boyd's ideas, companies can improve their operation, along with a board of directors that, if these bodies are well-composed and have an adequate style of work, allows:

> a) Improving the ability to "observe" what happens in the company and in the market, and
>
> b) Acting in an agile manner.

Consequently, if a company is able to better "capture" what is happening around it, it can react better and thus break the inertia more effectively.

As the experience of many companies has shown, company errors are largely consequences of decisions made, not so much of circumstances. Unlike models based on observing nature, companies that fail to adapt in time do not do so because they were unable but because they did not want to, or because they did not decide to act in time: they were victims of negative inertia.

Most of the decisions made within companies are based on dynamics that can be improved, especially with the support of a board that is actively focused and dedicated to govern the company, that is, a board of directors with a vigilant attitude.

Single-loop and double-loop learning [63]

"For Argyris and Schön learning involves the detection and correction of error. Where something goes wrong, it is suggested, an initial port of call for many people is to look for another strategy that will address and work within the governing variables. In other words, given or chosen goals, values, plans and rules are operationalized rather than questioned. According to Argyris and Schön (1974), this is *single-loop learning*. An alternative response is to question to governing variables themselves, to subject them to critical scrutiny. This they describe as *double-loop learning*. Such learning may then lead to an alteration in the governing variables and, thus, a shift in the way in which strategies and consequences are framed.

> *When the error detected and corrected permits the organization to carry on its present policies or achieve its presents objectives, then that error-and-correction process is single-loop learning. Single-loop learning is like a thermostat that learns when it is too hot or too cold and turns the heat on or off. The thermostat can perform this task because it can receive information (the temperature of the room) and take corrective action.*
>
> *Double-loop learning occurs when error is detected and corrected in ways that involve the modification of an organization's underlying norms, policies and objectives.*

Double-loop learning entails the modification of goals or decision-making rules in the light of experience. The first loop uses the goals or decision-making rules, the second loop enables their modification, hence "double-loop". Double-loop learning recognizes that the way a problem is defined and solved can be a source of the problem[64].

---

[63] http://infed.org/mobi/chris-argyris-theories-of-action-double-loop-learning-and-organizational-learning/

[64] https://en.wikipedia.org/wiki/Double-loop_learning

"Double-loop learning 'involves questioning the role of the framing and learning systems which underlie actual goals and strategies. In many respects the distinction at work here is the one used by Aristotle, when exploring technical and practical thought. Single-loop involves following routines and some sort of preset plan – and is both less risky for the individual and the organization, and affords greater control. The latter is more creative and reflexive, and involves consideration notions of the good. Reflection here is more fundamental: the basic assumptions behind ideas or policies are confronted... hypotheses are publicly tested... processes are "dis-confirmable" not self-seeking."[65]

The double bind

"When employees adhere to a norm that says "hide errors," they know they are violating another norm that says "reveal errors." Whichever norm they choose, they risk getting into trouble. If they hide the error, they can be punished by the top if the error is discovered. If they reveal the error, they run the risk of exposing a whole network of camouflage and deception. The employees are thus in a double bind, because whatever they do is necessary yet counterproductive to the organization, and their actions may even be personally abhorrent."[66]

Radar for companies' governance, by vigilant boards of directors

In the context in which there is now the challenge of governing companies in the era of acceleration; in which it has become necessary to be able to react to changes that are generated at increasing speeds, is that I suggest the idea of implementing a kind of "RADAR", tuned in a particular way for each and every company.

---

[65] http://infed.org/mobi/chris-argyris-theories-of-action-double-loop-learning-and-organizational-learning/
[66] https://hbr.org/1977/09/double-loop-learning-in-organizations

> *If you want different results,*
> *do not do the same things.*
> *Albert Einstein*

As we saw in Chapter II, the opportunities and difficulties of the digital age require the development of mechanisms capable of learning faster and performing better in terms of administration.

If the board a) does not want to be running the business with their vision trained on the past, b) does not want to depend only on the information received from administration, and c) does not want to be satisfied with itself in terms of successes already won – that is, looking at the dairy cows in the rearview mirror – they must then create a tool that allows them to look ahead.

The term *radar* comes from the English phrase "radio detection and ranging," which means detection and measurement of distance by radio. Using the analogy of navigation at sea, radar can be used to detect "contacts" that may pose risks for the ship, and to support navigation when it is near the coast.

From the radar operator's and navigator's points of view, the information provided by radar will help the person who runs the vessel to take the actions necessary for maintaining a safe course (assuming that it is sailing in deep waters), allowing it to reach the set destination. The frequency with which they review the information obtained from radar, and with which they take actions, is linked to the risk associated with the place and circumstances where they are navigating.

The objective of radar for the board will then be to help to:

- Detect opportunities not identified by administration in the strategic plan and threats not identified by administration in the strategic plan
- Identify the opportunities and threats on which to focus
- Monitor the conditions that have been identified
- Avoid single loop learning trap

- Avoid double bind trap

By emulating the help offered by radar to those responsible for a vessel's governance, the author's proposal is for each board to generate its own evaluation system to detect the opportunities and risks inherent to its company (called radar) that allows them even to identify the need to change the strategic plan on time.

The idea proposed is that this system of detection and monitoring for the board is composed of two "species" of "spider graphs" that record the position and sense of progress of the elements defined in two large areas: the more immediate one, called Level 1, and the more distant one, called Level 2:

- At level 1, the basic functions of good corporate governance, some of which will be reiterated later in this chapter, should be tracked or monitored. These correspond to what has "traditionally" been part of good corporate governance practices. So, since they are known and therefore easier to track and detect, I suggest that their position and sense of progress should be recorded closer to the center. In addition, the damage that can generate to the company the impact of a possible failure, should not take long to arrive.
- At level 2, the evolution of elements that the company needs in order to face the acceleration seen in the digital era should be tracked. Although they are crucial for survival in the medium- and long-terms for the company, they are represented as being farther from the center than level 1 elements, given that the company could operate in the short-term without them and because they can also be more difficult to detect.

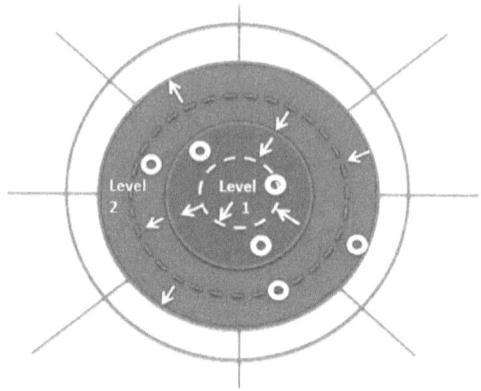

The linear composition of radar would incorporate monitoring elements that are considered relevant, along with the evaluation of their tendencies, such as those shown below (just as a very general example):

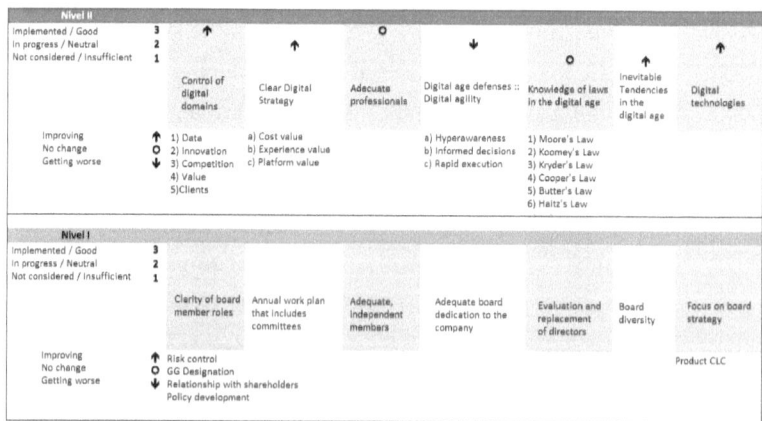

The risk of not implementing radar

If the board of directors continue to operate in the age of acceleration the same way as they did before and do not develop their own tool to "help good governance," they will be subject to suffering at least the following consequences:

a) Circularity: the boards will continue to make decisions based on the information and the approach provided only by administration. Given this, it will be difficult for them to see what the administration does not see.

b) Decide based on information from the past: it will be easier for boards to continue making use of the information generated by administration, which is typically based on previous data such as accounting, sales records, audits, etc. Given this, it will be difficult to break the pattern of continuing not to look in the rearview mirror.

Important elements to consider at Level 2

Given that the elements associated with what I have named Level 1 are known, I will continue by first complementing what is indicated in Chapter II with other topics that I consider useful when helping boards to define the critical elements to be monitored and evaluated in its respective level 2.

The Cows must feed Stars

In the age of acceleration, companies achieve a dynamic balance between *operating* current revenue-generating capabilities and *exploring* new businesses, which typically initially incur expenses.

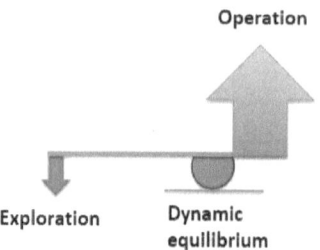

It is necessary to understand that what drives digital transformation is not only technology but a kind of *interaction between technology and strategy*; there may be multiple equilibrium positions, which are also dynamic and are in turn associated with *transitory successes*.

Dynamic equilibrium can be likened to riding a bicycle: to maintain balance, you have to keep moving. The point of balance that the company selects then corresponds to one of the alternatives of *dynamic equilibrium* and must be adjusted according to market reality, to the company, and to the products and services both in operations and in exploration.

With this logic, it is not possible to define a recipe to determine the percentage of the revenue that should be assigned to exploration. That number should be a matter of analysis, keeping in mind that there are in fact two important risks or possible pitfalls to avoid, in order to avoid falling into:

> 1. The *experimentation trap*, which occurs when over-investing in exploration.
>
> 2. The *competition trap*, which occurs when over-investing in operations.

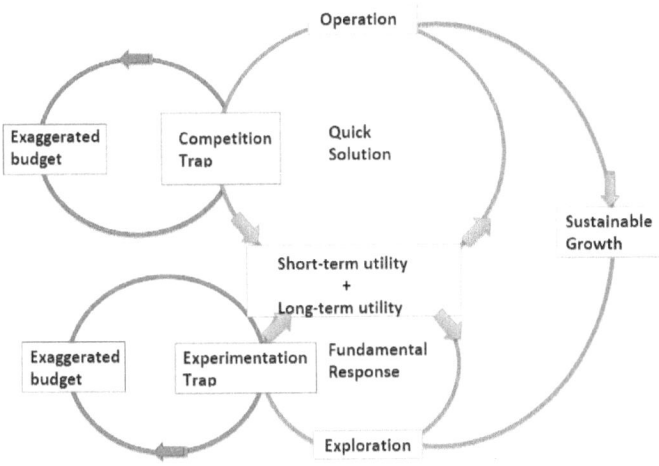

Using the objective of achieving sustainable growth as a reference, the company basically has two alternatives to balance:

- The quick solution is to emphasize the operation of current capabilities, hoping to generate short-term profits and taking the precaution of not falling into the competition trap.
- The fundamental response is to invest resources in exploration, with the hope of generating profits in the medium- and long-term, and taking precautions not to fall into the exploration trap.

Since exploration is associated with investments in research and development, experimentation, etc., it must be controlled by the board since management focused on the short-term and/or dazzled by the digital age may prefer to generate higher profits in the short-term, reducing R&D investments to the detriment of their future competitive position.

Stars are not born alone; they are "created" in the "space of questions."

As Clayton Christensen says in "How will you measure your life?": [67]

> If a company has ignored investing in new businesses until it needs those new sources of revenue and profits, it's already too late. It's like planting saplings when you decide you need more shade. It's just not possible for those trees to grow large enough to create shade overnight. It takes years of patient nurturing to have any chance of the trees growing tall enough to provide it.

One of the situations that you want to avoid is having a company that, following its strategic plan, achieves excellent results, then is left out of the market within a few years because of not knowing how to properly explore; just as – from a certain perspective – happened to Kodak and Nokia.

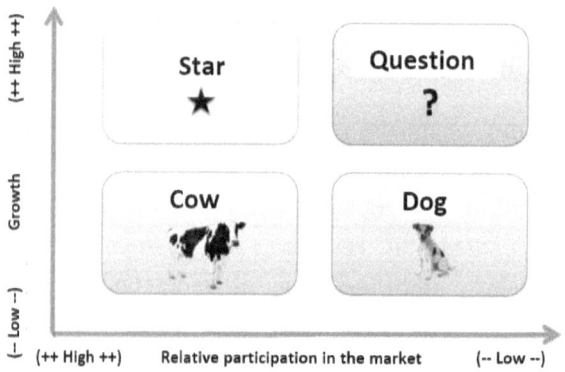

In 2014, the BCG revised its famous "Growth Matrix," also known as the "BCG Matrix," [68] the same one mentioned in the introduction that concludes the following:

---

[67] C. Christensen. J. Allworth & K. Dillon. How will you measure your life? HarperCollins. 2012

[68] https://www.bcg.com/publications/2014/growth-share-matrix-bcg-classics-revisited.aspx

- Companies moved through the matrix quadrants faster in the five-year period from 2008 to 2012 than in the five-year period from 1988 to 1992.
- The relationship between market share and sustained competitiveness were no longer valid.

Recommendations offered by the BCG, regarding the use of the Matrix 2.0:

Accelerate. It is critical to evaluate the portfolio frequently. Companies must increase the speed of their strategic clock to match that of the environment, with shorter planning cycles and feedback loops that require simplified approval processes for investment and divestment decisions.

Balance exploration and operation. This requires having an adequate number of questions and, at the same time, maximizing the benefits of cows as well as pets:

- Increase the amount of (?)
- Try the (?) quickly and efficiently
- Milk cows efficiently
- Keep pets on a short leash

Select rigorously. Companies must select investments and divestments carefully. Successful companies take advantage of a wide range of data sources and develop predictive analyses to determine which questions should be broadened through increased investment and which pets and cows they should sell proactively.

Measure and manage the economics of the experimentation portfolio. Understanding the level of experimentation required to maintain growth is important for long-term sustainability:

- Manage the rate of experimentation

- Promote the success of new products
- Maintain a balanced portfolio

If you want the company to have sustainable development and growth, you must keep investing and/or exploring with the aim of ensuring that your Stars (★) and Question Marks (?) can generate the resources necessary to replace cows and pets that are about to end their useful life.

The company's board must ensure that administration has defined and is executing an adequate balance between the use of current resources and the exploration of new opportunities in a way that allows the company to be profitable and sustainable, both in the short-term and in the future.

Steps needed to execute digital transformation [69]

Generate Value
The focus of effort must be oriented towards the use of digital technologies to transform or create processes or businesses where more value can be obtained.

Change the measurement of success
In the digital world, tests must be done in order to fail and learn quickly. One of the obstacles facing digital transformation comes from a structural problem, in that many companies basically use technology as an element of control and support –through an ERP, for example –as

---

[69] Arnuncio, Pablo (1 Jul 2018). "El rol del directorio en la transformación digital." From https://www.google.com.uy/search?q=Pablo+Arnuncio+de+EY.+El+Mercurio+1+de+Julio+2018.+Rol+del+Directorio+en+la+transformaci%C3%B3n+digital.&oq=Pablo+Arnuncio+de+EY.+El+Mercurio+1+de+Julio+2018.+Rol+del+Directorio+en+la+transformaci%C3%B3n+digital.&aqs=chrome..69i57.1325j0j7&sourceid=chrome&ie=UTF-8

it is the administration that is turned over to the person getting paid and taking measures not to take risks: the Administration and Finance Manager. The new paradigm to "fail quickly and learn quickly" requires that success no longer be measured by the mistakes that were made, but rather by the objectives that were reached and the new businesses that will be developed with the learning obtained.

Put the focus on people
Although the digital transformation makes changes in the way of working, the first cannot be achieved without a cultural change in the company. Therefore, the focus must remain on the people and on the steps necessary for carrying out changes.

Harness the power of data
Companies generate data in different ways and in different places, machines and systems. The challenge in the digital age is to take advantage of this huge amount of data to generate value, increase productivity, make better decisions, and create new businesses as well.

Develop collaborator networks
The speed and opportunities associated with the digital age make it difficult to think that the company is self-sufficient; therefore, new capacities must be generated through the creation of new associations and ways of collaborating.

Recognizing negative dynamics on boards

Understanding that the board of directors is the governance body of the company, it is essential for it to work properly. By this logic, professors Katharina Pick and Kenneth Merchant state that there are six tensions inherent to board operation, which, although they are particularly difficult and relevant to operation, [70] must exist in a moderated way:

a)   Stress of social cohesion
b)   Stress of discord
c)   Stress of psychological security
d)   Stress of collective feelings
e)   Stress of diverse thought
f)   Stress of a strong leader

In addition to the above, the same professionals mentioned signal the importance of recognizing the pathologies from which boards may suffer and that should be avoided:

a)   Excessive conformity
b)   Negative group conflict
c)   Politicking and formation of a dysfunctional coalition
d)   Habitual routines
e)   Bias towards shared information
f)   Pluralist ignorance
g)   Social laziness
h)   Group polarization

The researchers in question indicate that, in order to effectively manage board operation, its leaders and members must first understand the pathologies, their symptoms, and their causes. These could be the main cause of almost all failures in corporate governance, many of which were evident in the last decade.

What makes the treatment of these pathologies more problematic is that they cannot be eliminated entirely. By eliminating one pathology,

---

[70] Pick, Katharina and Merchant, Kenneth (2012). "Six Recognizing Negative Boardroom Group Dynamics." Chapter VI. In: Lorsch, Jay "The Future of Boards: Meeting the Governance Challengers of the Twenty-first Century." Harvard Business School Publishing Corporation.

it is usually causes another to become more prominent. The reality is that managing the dynamics of a board requires constant juggling to keep all the elements aligned so that the board is effective in meeting its most important current requirements.

Recognizing the business cycle of the products and services offered

Professors Jarden Harris and Michael Lenox have developed a simple tool called Competitive Life Cycle (CLC) [71] analysis of the business cycle in a dynamic market, which permits locating different products and services in three phases:

- Stage 1: Emerging, which goes on to the next stage after market recognition.
- Stage 2: Growth, in which revenues and, along with them, competition grows, until the prices are reduced and there is finally a shock in the market through which a few suppliers eventually remain.
- Stage 3: Growth is also possible, but it is typically slower and at the cost of taking the market away from competition, which typically leads to a reduction in margins. This stage ends when the product is replaced by another of superior technology or by a different concept; an example is the sale of CDs versus subscriptions to Spotify or Pandora.

---

[71] Harris, Jared and Lenox, Michael (2013). "The Strategist's Toolkit." Darden Business Publishing.

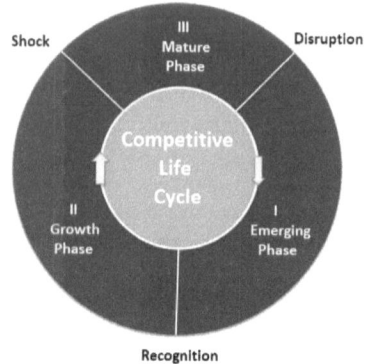

Important elements to consider at Level 1

Even if the elements associated with Level 1 are known, a review of the primary issues that must be taken into consideration follows.

Corporate Governance

I think it is important to begin by clarifying the origin of the term "corporate governance." Professor PhD Alfredo Enrione of the ESE Business School explains the origin of the term "corporate governance," [72] indicating that it comes from English and that its meaning refers to exercising control (governance) over a corporation. He himself proposes a definition that seems appropriate to me and that I would like to share with readers:

> "A set of processes, mechanisms, and rules of the game established among the owners, the board of directors, and the administration to manage the company, achieve set objectives, generate sustainable value over time for its

---
[72] Enrione, Alfredo (2014). "Directorio y Gobierno Corporativo: el desafío de agregar valor en forma sostenida." ESE Business School.

> *shareholders, and respond to the legitimate demands of other stakeholders."*

Next, I think it is important to answer the question, "What is a board?" by saying that it is only a group of people chosen by company shareholders to carry out the governance of the latter – not its administration.

To this I will add one of the reasons why companies should have a good board that is intelligent, skilled, or capable that can be the founding partner and/or manager, or whoever is in charge of leading the company administration:

- It provides complementary capabilities: a board should contribute those capabilities that complement those of the company manager.
- It establishes norms that form a Corporate Governance and with these creates the "balance" between the expectations of the different shareholders.
- It contributes independently to supervise and advise the administration, always watching over company interests.
- It establishes the strategic direction of the company.
- It legitimates the company and gives it credibility in the eyes of the market.

Generalizing even more and using experience from the world of large corporations, where property is typically atomized into many small shareholders (those who must appoint a manager to manage the company), I think it is appropriate to quote Professor B. Joseph White, [73] who thinks that the board is the body that helps solve a problem caused by competing interests. This is because the objective of the owners – the shareholders – is to maximize the value of the company and protect the value of its assets; meanwhile, the mangers' interest is maximizing their income – their compensation – and satisfying the multiple actors with whom they interact. Given that both interests compete for the same resources, in their vision, the role of the board is to:

a) Ensure that the shareholders' interest is above the manager's, ensuring the correct use of company resources.

b) Align the interests of shareholders and managers by designing a compensation plan based on performance, which ensures that the manager wins when the company wins.

Nowadays, we can see a variety of different realities when it comes to Business Governance issues:

- Those where the same person is the president and CEO, and/or the owner of 100% of the shares of the company is the president and general manager, so that the same person is performing both the role of governance and administration unchecked.
- Others where the manager has part of the property, sharing the role of Governance and holding on to that of administration.
- Those where the manager has no relevant shareholding and certainly has a board dedicated to governance issues.

Traditional vision of the environment in which companies live

Every company finds itself immersed in an environment where it coexists with a series of actors who go beyond customers and suppliers, thereby being influenced by entities such as the following: special interest groups, government and congress, labor regulations,

---

[73] White, Joseph (2014). "Do The Right Things: The Substance of Great Governance." In: Boards that Excel: candid insights and practical advice for directors. Chapter 4. Berrett-Koehler Publishers.

technical regulations, tax regulations, competent regulating bodies, banks, etc.

In the case of companies that have clients and suppliers of different nationalities, they are also exposed to the actions and demands of the respective governments to which said companies belong.

Therefore, the complexity to which companies are subjected can be so weighty as to make it advisable that, on one hand, they incorporate a board and, on the other, they make this organization work for the company's benefit, taking active measures to prevent it from running poorly or to eventually profit from the short-term on top of the long-term interest of the company (MDP).

Non-traditional vision of the environment in which companies live

Companies operate in an increasingly complex world, given that the business environment has become more diverse, dynamic, and interconnected than ever and is therefore less predictable.

According to Reed, Levin and Ueda's proposal, [74] companies should be disappearing faster than ever at a rate 6 times higher than 40 years ago. Behind this spike in "death rate" would be the inability to adapt to an increasingly complex environment, brought about by the following causes:

    1. Companies are facing the most diverse environment ever seen.
    2. Technological advances have increased the pace and impact of change.
    3. Companies are more interconnected than ever.

Role of the board of directors

---

[74] Reeves, Martín; Levin, Simon and Ueda, Daichi. (Jan-Feb 2016). "The Biology of Corporate Survival." Harvard Business Review. From https://hbr.org/2016/01/the-biology-of-corporate-survival

Although there are no apparent commandments for the role that the boards play in the environment described above – both per the traditional view and the non-traditional –, at least for companies not open on the stock exchange, the following three are commonly accepted as their minimum obligations:

- Advise the manager
- Support making complex decisions
- Monitor compliance with adopted agreements

But strictly speaking and using the "formal" corporate experience of open companies, the board of directors must "govern" the company. This implies, among other things, that it is the body responsible to shareholders for the proper operation of the company, and that its role goes far beyond giving advice and support.

Therefore, there are other activities that must be incorporated into the board's list of responsibilities to ensure the proper operation of a company, particularly in medium-sized companies:

- Control company strategy
- Ensure proper administration of the company, taking measures to avoid errors due to mishandling operations
- Ensure that there is a succession plan for the general manager and/or develop one
- Manage company risk
- Check compliance with current legal regulations
- Ensure the implementation of control mechanisms for conflicts between shareholders, be they first, second, or third generation (children, grandchildren, etc.)
- Renew board members, adapting to the needs of the company
- Appoint the general manager and define the executive compensation plan

Given the functions indicated, for a board to work properly it should then comply with at least the following:

- It must have been well-formed, considering combining the complementary experiences of members who have significant ability.
- Its members must invest – beyond the mere board meeting – all the time necessary to understand the company's situation in depth.
- It must be able to act independently while understanding the company and its respective industry, without giving in to the ills that usually affect the behavior of groups.
- It must exercise its authority beyond giving advice.
- It must be responsible for its actions and omissions.

In order to fulfill its duties and from the organizational point of view, the board is hierarchically located above the general manager, as it is responsible for the selection, hiring, and evaluation of the latter. But it must be careful not to attempt to exercise "executive command" over the general manager's subordinates, or not to generate a bureaucratic environment.

In formal terms, and again based on the experience of large companies in corporate governance,[75] the board must comply with the following functions:

- Maintain the bond with shareholders and define results that must be achieved by the organization, as well as establish limits for its executives
- Develop necessary policies for guiding the organization
- Ensure the organization's performance, verifying that it is moving towards the results that it seeks to achieve and that it does so in compliance with established policies

---

[75] See Carver's Model: http://www.policygovernance.com/pg-corp.htm

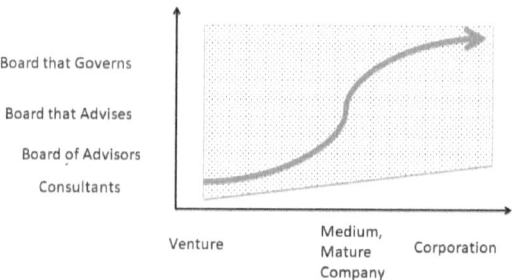

Types of boards and companies

Having said the above and considering the diverse reality faced by medium-sized companies – ranging from start-ups to mature companies with decades-long histories – I suggest accepting that, in practice, medium-sized companies can assign different roles to their boards as they go through different stages.

The roles assumed by the board of directors may change depending on the type of company, the level of participation that shareholders have in the administration, the level of development of the company, etc.

Thus, *companies that are not open to the stock market* could evolve over time, moving from having an advisor to going through a council of advisers to having a formal board, which goes beyond advising the general manager, as in the first two cases, to essentially governing the company.

In this way, the above picture attempts to visually synthesize the fact that different types of companies can assume different forms of governance. In the case of companies that are not open to the stock market (called medium-sized companies), it is common for their shareholders to have active participation both in the governance of the company and its management; its possible alternatives therefore ranges from having an advisory council to a board of directors that governs the company. The important thing for these companies is that the shareholders feel comfortable with the alternative put in place, whether that means having an advisory board or a board of directors that takes on the role of governing the company.

The board and resistance to change

It is common to hear and see that organizations, and the people that make them up, resist change.

It is easy to be tempted to believe that resistance to change only comes from company workers. But what happens when resistance to change also comes from the manager, the founding partner, or even the chairman of a company's board of directors? What organization has the capacity to avoid a collapse, in addition to the failure that the market can provoke? In fact, there are numerous examples of companies that achieved remarkable successes breaking into markets dominated by actors that had formidable "positions" and, on their way to success, dethroned those who were once leaders.

Undoubtedly, the board has a role to play in the ability to detect and protect the company from the harm that resistance to change can cause. In addition, it has the power and obligation to act in a timely manner.

Focus that the board should have

If companies do not live a static reality, boards should also continually adapt their work, their approach, and their capabilities to the requirements per the "stage of life" that the company is going through.

With the Adizes model, described in the next chapter, as a reference, it could be said that, in the early stages associated with the growth period, the company's executive team will probably require more support to manage the "disorder" inherent to its growth, in order to be sure to comply with regulations and to adopt good practices aimed at defining roles and separating functions. It will also have to face the adaptation of the founder's role and possibly get the participation of family members and others in order.

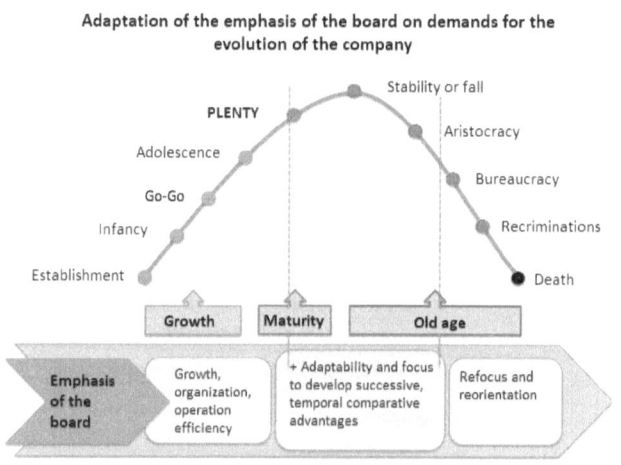

Adaptation of the emphasis of the board on demands for the evolution of the company

In the mature period, the company will face problems that it has not faced before. It will run the risk of "resting on its laurels," of becoming rigid, of not continuing to innovate, of losing the "entrepreneurial drive," etc. The board must then anticipate these risks, doing whatever necessary to turn the risks into opportunities and to keep the company in the "state of plenty."

Finally, if the company leaves the stage of plenty and enters the phase of old age, or if the company has experienced an external "shock" of proportions such as that suffered by Kodak and Fujifilm in the photography industry, the board should face a new sequence of stages, each one more difficult to reverse than the previous, and it will have to face the challenge of restoring the company to the state of plenty.

Sources of information for the board

The information that directors have will serve as a basis for decision-making. A problem that may arise is linked to the fact that – at least in the corporate world – the reports that directors receive are prepared by the company's executive staff, which, assuming that it is composed of honest and hard-working people, will have a tendency to highlight the good. In fact, even hard-working people can "disguise" or inadequately justify negative aspects of the operation in addition to highlighting the good.

Given this, the boards should, beyond just reviewing reports submitted by management, at least:

- Validate the sources of the information
- Make use of audited accounting
- If necessary, request for new information be incorporated
- Define how often the information is presented in a manner consistent with the administrative capabilities of the company

Board relationship with executives

For a board to be effective, it must be able to maintain a delicate balance in the relationship with company executives. They must have a challenging and critical attitude on one hand and a supportive attitude on the other.

The boards can form work committees to advance on specific issues beyond board meetings. These committees can report their progress to the board and should feel free to meet without the general manager present.

Some of the most common committees are indicated below, and there may be others depending on the type of company and the industry in which they work:

Strategy	Auditing	Investigation
Finances	Risk	Marketing
Compensation	Ethics	Public Relations
Investments	Security	Norm Compliance

Involvement of the board in company strategy

Boards must be able to identify, react to, and ideally anticipate changes that may affect the industry in which the company operates. In the example given in the introduction, the wrong reaction to an external "shock" that Kodak implemented was discussed. Below, a brief summary of Fujifilm's successful and heterogeneous response is presented.

Fujifilm versus Kodak. Public companies that faced the "shock" of digital technology with a different approach.

Those who were born prior to the year 2000 may remember that, on entering a photography shop, there were typically yellow and green boxes that held rolls of film belonging to two large manufacturers, Kodak and Fujifilm.

"Fuji Photo Film" was founded in 1934 in a small city located at the foot of Mount Fuji in Japan, with the aim of being the first Japanese producer of photographic film. Through carrying out a sustained effort in this region for the next ten years, the company reached national production of photographic and cinematographic films and printing X-ray films. In the 1940s, "Fuji Photo" entered the market of optical glasses, lenses, and equipment. After the World War II, the company promoted diversification, entering the fields of medicine (X-ray diagnostics), printing, electronic imaging, and magnetic materials. In 1962, Fuji Photo and the British company Rank Xerox Limited (now Xerox Limited), launched Fuji Xerox Co. Ltd., a "joint venture."

Since the mid-1950s, Fuji Photo has accelerated establishing international sales bases. With the aim of launching its Fujifilm brand internationally in the 1980s, Fuji Photo expanded production and other bases abroad, accelerating the pace of its business's globalization. However, Fuji Photo led the industry in developing digital technologies to be used in companies related to photography, medicine, and printing. These technologies allowed Fuji Photo to become a driving force in the development of these markets. Fujifilm and Kodak serve as an example to consider that, beyond the external origin of the threat, it was the "internal response" that made the difference.

As indicated in a previous example, the "Eastman Kodak Company," better known as Kodak, started as the "Eastman Dry Plate Company" founded by inventor George Eastman and Henry Strong in 1888. Its great commercial success began with the commercialization of the paper reel in 1888 – moving away from the use of glass plates used until then – and the market introduction of what was an innovative camera in those years, the Kodak 100 Vista, which used circular reels of 100 photos instead of a plate. Kodak successfully managed to make photography simple and was known by the slogan, "You press a button, we do the rest."

The photography industry suffered a crisis at the end of the 1990s when digital photography reached the consumer market, quickly impacting the demand for rolls of film. Unlike Kodak, Fujifilm responded with a series of radical reforms[76] aimed at diversifying the business by associating with companies, investing in R & D, and buying about 40 companies; it not only explored alternatives that could have been considered to be in "adjacent markets," but it also opened its analysis to completely new business areas, such as pharmaceuticals and cosmetics, since through them it could take advantage of its strengths in chemistry and materials. The "traditional" photography market reached its peak in the year 2000, and over the next ten years it shrunk by 90%, leading Kodak to declare bankruptcy under Chapter 11 on January 11, 2012; during this period, Fujifilm – unlike Kodak – grew stronger as a solid business group.

Beyond the strategies implemented by both companies to face the shock of digitalization in the traditional photography market – whose analysis is not the focus of this book – the difference in the approaches implemented by the leaders of Fujifilm and Kodak serves as an example to consider that, beyond the external origin of the threat, it was the "internal response" that made the difference.

Thus, a significant part of why companies do not reach their maximum potential development could be linked to "inadequate driving." That is, even when it seems contradictory or counterintuitive, a company that achieved what Dr. Adizes would call maturity, if it does not become a victim of *paralyzing* or *blinding inertia*, should be able to react to any adverse situation, survive it, and ideally turn it into an opportunity, as Fujifilm did.

This does not mean that the only cause of bad driving linked to strategic errors committed by *paralyzing* or *blinding inertia*. Quite the contrary, a company is a complex organization, and reaching its maximum potential development requires good management in the multiple areas of which it is comprised, that is, in organizational, operational, commercial, productive, financial, and R & D aspects, and so on.

Although these two companies faced the same external "shock," the reactions were radically different, such that that Kodak ended a long

---

[76] Reeves, Martin; Levi, Simon and Ueda, Daichi (January-February 2016). "The Biology of Corporate Survival." Harvard Business Review.

period of agony by filing for bankruptcy in 2012, while Fujifilm is still a very successful company; this suggests the importance of board involvement in company strategy. Boards should avoid the pathologies, such as "excessive compliance," that may affect them.

The boards are not called on to attend mere monthly meetings about balance reviews or to become *mailboxes* for the strategic plan presented by company management. On the contrary, directors must:

- Prepare the succession of the CEO / general manager
- Work together with management to develop a strategic plan
- Follow its convictions
- Identify innovations that may be disruptive with enough time to react
- Monitor the correct execution of the strategy
- Protect the company as necessary from bad decisions eventually made even by its founders

For those who think that preparing the succession of the manager may not seem like an important issue, I tell them that, according to Eben Harrell,[77] every year between 10% and 15% of the corporations must appoint a new CEO (Chief Executive Officer or general manager) due to various reasons such as retirement, resignation, health problems, etc. In addition, according to a survey conducted by *Heidrick & Struggles* and the *Rock Center for Corporate Governance* at Stanford University, only 54% of boards are preparing a specific candidate and 39% do not have a viable internal candidate capable of replacing the general manager, should the need arise.

Independence of directors

Beyond what law establishes in different countries and certainly, in addition to this, directors are elected by the owners or shareholders to govern companies. It is by this logic that directors, rather than

---

[77] Harrell, Eben (December 2016). "Succession Planning: What the Research Says." Harvard Business Review.

worrying about representing the shareholder(s) who appointed them, must act for the benefit of the company, even when this means disagreeing with the shareholder that chose them. This is because it is ultimately the company that shareholders want to protect.

To understand the previous paragraph, the reader can think of the following analogy: when visiting a doctor, even if he selects the professional and pay, it will be the doctor who will give a diagnosis and determine treatment. These actions will be guided by the doctor's technical knowledge and interest in the patient's health, not by pleasing the patient's preference, who might not be interested in recognizing that he has a specific ailment and/or accepting that he needs a treatment that he might not like.

The oft-mentioned "independence" of directors should not be understood only in that they should not be linked to a competing company, because if it were, they would lack the most basic professional ethics which could constitute an "interlocking "between competing companies, a practice that could become illegal. In this way, independence must be accepted, as a true authorization for each director to think and decide conscientiously based on what he believes is the best for the company.

To truly have companies that surpass the growth stage and arrive and remain in a *state of plenty*, the fact that directors are also independent of the owners – to the company's benefit – will be one of the most effective "insurances" that the shareholders themselves will have to protect their own interest: the continuity and the good of their company.

Unfortunately, achieving independence of directors from the owners that appoint them is a difficult thing to achieve. This is because, particularly in complex matters or those related to family issues, egos, etc., there is an incentive on the part of the director chosen not to disagree with the shareholder who chose him to therefore avoid conflicts.

Although the topic of board dynamics is not addressed in this book, those who wish to learn more on the subject can find information in Chapter V of my book *"Gobierno Corporativo para la Mediana Empresa"*. In this regard, it can be said that independent directors are faced with a series of risks and difficulties, among which it helps to highlight the following:

- It can take years to acquire a profound knowledge of the company that allows them to become a real contribution
- Independent directors are more dependent than "internal" directors on the information provided by management

Some famous founders who were fired from their companies

One of the reasons why I believe that directors should look after the good of the company and be involved in its strategy, besides worrying about representing shareholders, may be seen in cases where the board removed those who were founding partners from their positions.

Clearly, the idea of this book and the board of directors is not to act against the general manager, and less so when the latter is the company's founder. But for reference, and to be consistent with reality, below I cite several cases of widely known companies where the board had to request the departure of one of its founding partners from company management.

1. Steve Jobs, co-founder of Apple. The iconic Apple man was not always the face of the company he co-founded in 1976. Jobs was forced to leave Apple in 1985 after a fight with the board of directors. He returned in 1996 to serve as interim CEO and became permanent CEO in 1997 after Apple bought NeXT, the company he founded while he was away from Apple.

2. Mike Lazaridis, founder of Research In Motion (RIM). Lazaridis, a pioneer in smartphone technology, was a co-founder of Research In Motion, which manufactured the BlackBerry. Lazaridis resigned from the role of CEO in 2012. While there were rumors that his "retirement" was due to pressure from shareholders, the fact is that he left the company entirely after the launch of BlackBerry 10, a smartphone that the company expected compete with the iPhone.

3. Jerry Yang, co-founder of Yahoo! This was a pioneer of Internet search engines in the late 1990s, but it struggled to stay relevant when facing giants such as Google and Facebook. It was in this climate and in the midst of criticism for rejecting a Microsoft purchase offer for $47.5 billion USD that the board fired Yang as CEO in 2008. Yang started the company in 1995 and remained involved until he was completely separated.

4. Martin Eberhard, co-founder of Tesla

5. Aubrey McClendon, founder of Chesapeake

6. Andrew Mason, founder of Groupon

7. David Neleman, founder of JetBlue

Dedication to the company

The survey developed by McKinsey and the Canada Pension Plan Investment Board – whose main results were cited at the start of this chapter – makes the fragile functioning of many boards clear. Several of the cases of private companies described coincide in the lack of understanding had by the boards, at least in cases where companies had boards.

Just as a reference for shareholders seeking to review the functioning of their boards, I present the following table[78] developed by Harvard Business School professor Jay W. Lorsch and consultant Colin B. Carter, in which dedication is correlated in the number of days that directors should dedicate to the companies, along with the style of the board and the situation of the company:

	Board Style	
	Observer	Challenging
Situation of the company and complexity of the industry — Demanding	20 days a year	40 days a year
Situation of the company and complexity of the industry — Stable and satisfactory	10 days a year	20 days a year

As a complement to the table shown, and given the fact that there seems to be no single criterion regulating the dedication required to achieve proper board functioning, I summarize other considerations that can typically be of use when organizing a board:

a) To achieve good operations, it is not enough for a board to be made up of suitable members. This body must invest the time necessary to understanding the company's reality.

b) There are radically different realities for the different types of companies, so references of companies at the same level of billing or in

---

[78] Lorsch, Jay y Carter, Colin (2003). "Back to the Drawing Board: Designing Corporate Boards for a Complex World." Chapter IV: Different roles for Different Boards. Harvard Business School Press.

101

the same industry should not be used when allocating the amount of time: each company must ensure that its board has a comprehensive understanding of the company and the industry in which it operates.

c) The experience that directors have, as well as a board's governance style, will also influence the time necessary for the board of directors to achieve a good level of understanding of the company and its environment.

Separation between the positions of board chairman and general manager

Although this is a subject in which there is no "consensus" or "norm," it seems important to raise some arguments behind the two main alternatives:

a)   Separation of office: the fact that the chairman of the board is not also the general manager prevents the creation of excess power, which facilitates everything from making mistakes in governance, to diverse types of abuse and even fraud, as has happened in countless companies. But for those who are not convinced of the benefit of separating the positions, I add that there is a *problem of circularity*, in which the same person who presides over the board of directors acts as the manager of the company and therefore determines the agenda of the board of directors, directs its meetings, assigns work, and gives feedback to the same directors; who in turn supervise the same manager, evaluate the same manager, define the compensation of the same manager, manage the succession of the same manager, and approve the proposals of the same manager.

b)   The fact that the chairman of the board is also the general manager allows the president and general manager to organize the board so that it can maneuver more quickly. Although it carries the risk indicated in the previous point, it reduces the danger of having board chairmen who are not sufficiently involved in the company.

Personally, I prefer the system in which the chairman of the board does not have the position of general manager, as long as there is a professional, well-formed board that operates effectively.

Replacement of directors

Replacing directors is another topic on which it is possible to find different solutions, as well as many omissions. As a measure to facilitate designing the most appropriate solution for each company, I would like to consider the following:

a) Directors must gain a high level of knowledge of the industry and the company in particular, so their terms should not be short; that is, they should not serve for less than 4 years, as a reference.

b) A mechanism must be established that allows directors to be replaced in a "pseudo-automatic" manner, that is, without the need to compromise the friendly relationship that normally occurs between owners and directors.

That said, there are different mechanisms that tend to facilitate the replacement of directors, some of which I indicate below:

a) Appointing directors for a fixed term without replacement (for example, for a period of four years): on one hand, it can be positive since it eliminates the painful step of the owners having to tell a friend that they should leave the board. It can be negative because they can lose valuable information and knowledge about the company.

b) Appointing directors for a fixed term with only one possible reelection: this is an alternative to the previous proposal with the only difference being that it incorporates the possibility of extending the stay of a director for another term, which can be considered to be very valuable. It may be negative in terms of discretionary use, which could generate conflicts with directors who are not asked to stay on for a second term.

c) Appointing directors for one-year terms with renewal: on one hand, this can be positive, as it allows the boards to be adjusting very quickly and flexibly in the face of changes. On the other hand, it can be negative if the owners do not dare, for whatever reason, to renew the stay of one member while retaining the rest.

Diversity

Diversity is a term that is often misinterpreted. Margaret Neale, professor and Chair of Organizations and Dispute Resolution at the Stanford Graduate School of Business, has made remarkable studies regarding diversity in the workplace:

> What you don't see is diversity having a direct performance effect," says Neale. It turns out that different types of diversity generate various sorts of conflict, which affects how a team performs. "The kind of group conflict that exists and how the team handles the conflict will determine whether this diversity is effective in increasing or reducing performance. [79]

At one extreme, if all the members of a board think in the same way, they will not be able to detect the problems and risks affecting the company. It is therefore convenient to consider that the board includes people who play complementary roles. A good way to achieve this goal is to have diverse members, and a practical way to "share" diversity is by incorporating women and other minorities on boards.

Given that, in the vast majority of cases, the board members are men, there are countries – particularly European – that have tended to incorporate legislation mandating the incorporation of women.

Although there is no consensus regarding the benefits that incorporating women can have for companies, the following is a table

---

[79] See: Stanford GSB Staff (1999). "Diversity and Work Group Performance." From https://www.gsb.stanford.edu/insights/diversity-work-group-performance

of regulations that are being implemented progressively in some European countries for boards of companies that are open on the stock exchange. [80]

Country	Quota of Women	Start Date	Companies Included
Belgium	1:3	2017	Large companies that trade on the stock exchange
France	40%	2017	Larger companies
Iceland	40%	2013	Public companies
Italy	33%	2011	Companies open to the stock exchange
Malaysia	30%	2016	Private companies
Holland	33%	2015	Companies open to the stock exchange and other large companies
Norway	40%	2009	Public companies on the stock exchange and other state companies
Spain	40%	2015	State companies

In addition to the above information, it may also be useful to analyze the number of women participating on boards in different countries:

---

[80] See: For more information see websites of: Government UK, Deloitte, UK Parliament, Europe:
https://www.gov.uk/government/uploads/system/upload/attachment_data/files/31480/11-745-women-on-boards.pdf

Country	%	Country	%
Norway	36,7	France	29,9
Sweden	24,4	Italy	22,3
Finland	22,1	Denmark	21,8
Belgium	18,3	Germany	18,3
South Africa	17,5	New Zealand	17,5
Netherland	17,3	Austria	16,3
Israel	16,2	United Kingdom	15,6
Australia	15,1	Ireland	14,4
Canada	13,1	Spain	12,5
United States	12,2	Luxemburg	11,5
Malaysia	10,4	Switzerland	10
Turkey	10	Thailand	9,7
Greece	9,6	Singapore	9
China	8,5	Hong Kong	8,4
India	7,7	Philipines	7,4
Colombia	7	Brazil	6,3
Mexico	6,2	Russian Fed.	5,7
Taiwan	4,9	Chile	3,8
Indonesia	3,7	Japan	2,4

Source: *Deloite, Women in the board room, 2015*

Board design

In order for a company to aspire to reach its maximum potential, it helps for it to design its board well. While the word "design" may seem exaggerated, I would like to clarify emphatically that it is not.

One of the common practices in medium-sized companies is that, when it or its owners decide to implement a board, they start by think of people by first and last names, rather than by defining the roles, along with the experience and knowledge needed so that the board can fulfill its functions.

It is important for the board to be made up of well-prepared individuals who understand the industry in which the company operates, that have useful, relevant experience, and that are in tune with the strategic challenges that the company is facing.

In fact, there are companies that provide consultation services in the design and subsequent constitution of boards.

Some of the roles that it may be useful to "cover" when defining the profile for a particular director might be the following:

- Business development
- Knowledge of the industry
- Knowledge of a certain process
- Financial experience
- Commercial experience
- Organizational experience
- Ability to understand the economy and the business environment
- Strategic experience
- Knowledge of international markets (where the company operates)

Another aspect that might seem "soft" but is not, and that I recommend considering when designing a board, is choosing external directors (not family members or executives) based on who, beyond having the abilities and independence needed, has the disposition required to act in a timely manner, speak sincerely, and express an opinion directly, even when the last of these does not align with the rest of the board's opinions.

If you really want your company to become know, select people who will tell you what you really do not see and need to know at the right time. Consider the ancient Chinese proverb that says:

> Elegant words are not sincere,
> sincere words are not elegant.
> *Lao Tsé*

Remuneration of directors

The remuneration of directors must be good enough relative to the time commitment required, but not so good that they are unwilling to step down.

Members of the same board must not necessarily have the same remuneration. For example, it might be advisable to have one very prestigious member whose remuneration is higher than that of the rest. If this is the case, my only recommendation is for this to be handled in an absolutely transparent manner.

Beyond the number of meetings, it is convenient to set a monthly remuneration, based on the fact that this is a fixed responsibility.

Adding extra remuneration for participation in certain committees may also be considered.

One element that allows the legal risk directors run to be reduced, and by which they can avoid paying an extra premium on expenses, is to purchase insurance for directors and executives known by their English acronym D & O, "directors and officers."

Different perspectives among directors

There are different perspectives on the boards that are valuable and that must be properly considered. [81] In fact, being a company director in which one participates in property is not the same as being a completely independent director. So that board members can understand that opinion can also depend on the position held in this governing body, it is helpful to consider the following:

- The board must recognize that there is no single structure that works in all cases.

---

[81] George, William (2012). "Board Governance depends on where you sit." Chapter 5. In: The Future of Boards: Meeting the Governance Challengers of the Twenty-First Century. Harvard Business Review Press.

- It is important that all parties, especially the executive director, recognize the different points of view of their members and seek to minimize conflicts arising from the perspective of the director's own position.
- It is recommended that the board presidents participate in other boards and ideally in different positions.

Complacency

One of the common attitudes of managers in the face of non-compliance with the goals approved by the board of directors, and which is sometimes accepted by the latter, is to blame "competitors" (the external origin of the threat), for which they usually provide arguments such as those given below:

Negative scope:

- The competition lowered prices
- The competition gives away services
- The competition brings in Chinese products or products manufactured in countries that do not meet international standards

Positive scope:

- The competition is second to none with the new line of products that it brought to the market
- The competition has a couple of star sellers
- The competition has been in the market for longer

I ask you to stop for a moment and consider the following question. How much do unforced errors affect the company's competitive advantage? What is the cost of this type of error? Asked in another way, how much money do you think could have been converted into company use if internal aspects had been handled better?

Rarely are other types of arguments heard, arguments related more to unfulfilled goals or the lower product usefulness for self-improvement opportunities or, lastly, errors committed within the company, such as the following:

- Internal operational errors
    - Delays in issuing invoices
    - Delays in the collection process
    - Poorly optimized credit structures
    - Bad handling of foreign currencies
    - Poorly chosen insurance
    - Personnel with expired licenses and documents
    - Staff with inadequate training plans
- Errors in price setting
    - High prices that reduce sales volume
    - Low prices that generate insufficient margins
    - Errors in the pricing policy of the service unit
- Errors in the advertising strategy
    - Inadequate segmentation
    - Inadequate mix of products and services
    - Lack of sales presence in the field
- Errors in the product development strategy
    - Lack of investment in innovation (research and development)
    - Poorly targeted resources for research and development
- Errors in the stock policy
    - Excess stock immobilized
    - Poor selection of inventories
    - Excess breakdown of products with high turnover
- Errors in logistics
    - Shipping costs for carrying the wrong product
    - Transportation costs for buying the wrong product
    - Transportation costs due to delayed payment of the purchase order

- - Air transportation costs for a product offered with immediate delivery and that was not in stock
- Strategic errors
  - Not (really) understanding real customers need
  - Not investing enough in exploring new business or new technologies
  - Not investing enough in advance in exploring new technologies or businesses
  - Not investing in training staff in relevant technologies or techniques

And the worst part is that board members are often not heard asking the questions that can identify problems such as those described, identify opportunities to improve the company's future results, and remunerate executives correctly, as well.

That is to say, there seems to be on one hand samples of a kind of conformism at the board level in some cases; on the other, it seems common to underestimate the potential for *extra utility* that is hidden inside the company and that only requires better management to be *unearthed*; it also seems that there is sometimes the idea – an incorrect one, by the way – that the competitive advantage had can be maintained *forever*.

Many managers and directors have heard about the continual improvement practices used in the Japanese automotive industry as a source of success they have achieved; however, in many cases, it seems that the interest in working toward continual improvement is relegated to the theoretical level in day-to-day operations.

Given the reality of the medium-sized companies on which this book focuses, the boards would produce a great contribution if they maintained an attitude that I call *vigilant* at an almost paranoid level. What I mean is that the board's way of working at least incorporates the spirit of continual improvement through "recursive" and periodic reviews done by specific committees.

The *strategic vigilant attitude* should be focused on anticipating situations related to the operation and changes that the market may observe in the future. It should be able to identify dangers associated with the innovation of competitors or with disruptive technologies that threaten the future of the company, as well as the eventual appearance of higher added value applications/solutions that may affect the company's current business. It must, then, ensure that innovation is managed properly to adapt the company's strategies and organization in order to maintain a competitive advantage.

The *operational vigilant attitude* should focus on finding improvement opportunities in internal work, which allows minimizing "self-inflicted" losses as much as possible, while at the same time maximizing processes as much as possible to make them more efficient and economical.

The *organizational vigilant attitude* should focus on controlling the structure and preparation (training) of company members so that it keeps up with adaptations of the strategic and operational requirements, as well as at which stage of evolution the company is. In addition, measures should be taken to avoid family conflicts and ensure that there is a plan for succession.

The *adaptive vigilant attitude* should focus on recognizing and facing new market requirements, as well as internal company factors capable of inhibiting responses or opportune reactions. I am referring to:

- Fear of change
- Lack of energy to implement changes
- Inability to recognize the need to change
- Refusal to change (a risk that commonly haunts founders who have already been successful)

A basic recommendation to express the work done by boards, and to make them more effective, is to generate an annual work calendar based on different types of activities, such as the following:

- Board meetings to review the company's situation
- Committee meetings
- Strategic review
- Operational review
- Etc.

Finally, I also suggest that the board analyze and consider promoting benefits associated with the so-called "founders' mentality," which are related to ways of reducing the complexity of growth as a means of avoiding the bureaucratization of the company, keeping costs down, and staying close to the sales line. [82]

Board meetings

Board meetings may occur on a bi-monthly or quarterly basis. Its functioning should be based on the report generated by management, delivered a couple of days in advance. The table with the topics to be discussed should also be sent in advance and be articulated by the chairman of the board of directors or a leader assuming this role, so that the directors can request the inclusion of topics that they consider relevant in time.

In these meetings, among other things, compliance with the annual plan (YTD year to date) should be reviewed, and the business plan for the following year should be approved before the end of the year (the fiscal year more so than the calendar year, when they do not coincide).

These meetings should also be attended by the entire board, the general manager, and the managers of main areas, as appropriate for the topics discussed in the table.

---

[82] Zook, Chris y Allen, James (2016). "The Founder's Mentality." Harvard Business Review Press.

Committee meetings

The committee meetings should be carried out as often as necessary, per the requirements of the moment in which the company finds itself and aiming to implement, monitor, and develop a kind of sequence of continual improvement by area.

In these meetings, the director who leads the committee should participate, along with the necessary executives and collaborators. It is not mandatory for the general manager to attend these meetings, nor for him to be a member of all the committees.

The conclusions or relevant information of these committees must be communicated to the rest of the directors so that it can be included in the report presented at the next board meeting.

Strategic review meetings

Strategic review meetings should be held at least once a year (ideally two or three times) and if you are going to have one, I suggest that it take place before the annual shareholders' meeting.

Participants in these meetings should be those that the director leading the committee deems necessary, but they should typically include area managers, in addition to the general manager, and an expert speaker on a subject relevant to the industry may also be incorporated.

Just to insist on the importance of the strategy, consider the words of Sun Tzu:

> Strategy without tactics
> is the slowest route to victory.
> Tactics without strategy
> is the noise before defeat.
> *Sun Tzu*

If you think that my suggestion to carry out several strategy reviews a year is exaggerated, I will tell you that MIT professor Donald N. Sull[83] points out that, in order to close the gap between strategy and its execution, we must abandon the traditional vision that considers strategy development to be a linear process, as this logic has at least three fatal errors: a) the linear view separates the formulation of strategy from its execution; b) it encourages leaders to develop a strategy even when it may be based on incorrect information; c) it ignores the importance of timing.

Instead of the vision of linear strategy, Professor Sull suggests considering an inherently iterative alternative by which the strategy is always in development and subject to revisions, in light of the interactions between the organization and the changing environment.

Finally, do not forget the words of the famous Marshal Helmuth Carl Bernard von Molke:

> No plan, no matter how good it is,
> resists the first contact with the enemy,
> with reality.

Operational review meetings

In mid-sized companies, operational review meetings should be held at least twice a year to verify that the company is on the path defined by the strategic plan and to correct any deviation that may have occurred as quickly as possible.

In my opinion, this work is so important that I would like to cite the opinion of a famous professor of strategy at Harvard Business School, *Michael Porter*, for whom "operational effectiveness and strategy are

---

[83] Sull, Donald. "Closing the Gap Between Strategy and Execution. Top 10 lessons on Strategy - MIT Sloan Management Review. SLOANSELECT COLLECTION

both essential to superior performance, which, after all, is the primary goal of any enterprise. But they work in very different ways."

Given the above, my suggestion is for operational efficiency to be given the importance it deserves. One way in this sense is to organize operational review meetings in which we, randomly and with the best "business sense" possible, analyze issues related to operational efficiency in various areas such as sales, acquisitions, finances, etc.

The table below serves as a reference for the way in which an annual calendar of activities could be viewed. Instead of indicating specific months, a relative nomenclature is used, since there are countries in which the "fiscal year" starts in January, others in July, others in October, etc.

Annual calendar of board activities												
	Month 1	Month 2	Month 3	Month 4	Month 5	Month 6	Month 7	Month 8	Month 9	Month 10	Month 11	Month 12
Director meeting			✓			✓			✓			✓
Committee meetings	✓	✓			✓		✓	✓		✓		
Strategic revision				✓								
Operational revision						✓						✓

Another possible alternative in medium-sized companies is incorporating sessions with different emphases in annual board planning, thus setting aside time to analyze particular issues that could have been specific to a committee.

"Vigilant" result statement and utility reserves

The participants in these operational review meetings should be those who the director leading the committee deems necessary, according to the topic being analyzed.

They should do the impossible of identifying procedures that allow "freeing" those "utility reserves" that are lost due to internal errors in the company. As a tool to support the objective at hand, I suggest incorporating the use of a modified result statement called *"vigilant EERR"* in which – by over-accounting – operational expenses that were the result of errors beyond what a normal operation would have had are separately identified:

EERR (Traditional)	*Vigilant* EERR
Sales earnings	Sales earnings
Sales expenses	Sales expenses
Gross margin	**Gross margin**
	Operations expenses
	Projected EBITDA
Operational errors expenses	Operational errors expenses
EBITDA Yielded	**EBITDA Yielded**
Depreciations and amortizations	Depreciations and amortizations
Operations utility	**Operations utility**
Financial expenses	Financial expenses
Pre-tax utility	**Pre-tax utility**
Taxes	Taxes
Net Utility	**Net Utility**

Attitude of the board towards inertia

The board must maintain a kind of fear (again, almost paranoid) of not being able to make the organization capable of reacting at the right speed to a new trend or change, since these can cause the company to lose its competitive advantage, or they can generate a new source of income.

Given the above, the board must develop and maintain a vigilant attitude capable of recognizing the eventual emergence or existence of *"negative" inertias* that could be affecting both the ability to identify changes and to react to them by implementing the necessary measures and doing so in time.

In the book *Building the Agile Business Through Digital Transformation*, Neil Perkin[84] summarizes something that boards should not forget:

> *If an organization has been increasing its operation and growing by using specific processes or specific ways of doing things, it will create an inertia that is very difficult to counteract. As the company gets bigger and the focus moves more towards efficiency and optimization instead of disruptive innovation, the ways of dealing with situations become entrenched. As hierarchies flourish within the company that is becoming increasingly larger and growing around its own practices, the company's internal focus is increasing while the outward focus decreases. The result: inertia strengthens over time.*

Attitude of the board of directors towards company employees

An important detail has to do with the attitude of the board of directors, which has to feel like an organization destined to work for the company. It should avoid creating an arrogant or self-serving attitude, especially toward those who are company employees: it is one thing to have the responsibility of governing and it is another to believe that the company can work just with directors (the era in which emperors were left behind). In all the companies that I have known, there are very valuable people carrying out operational functions with

---

[84] Neil Perkin. Building the Agile Business through Digital Transformation (page 35). Kindle edition.

a high level of dedication, which would, if carried out without this "affection," generate extra costs and damage for the company.

Therefore, while the board can and must be demanding, it must also show respect for the employees who work at the company, especially by showing sensitivity every time a report is requested or a meeting or any activity for the organization requires a collaborator's time.

Number of directors

There is no formula to determine the number of members a board must have. The number of directors depends on the complexity of the company, its size, the number of committees, the geographical area it covers, and the ability to find and pay good, dedicated directors.

Evaluation to be carried out by directors

Experiences in the corporate world could suggest the helpfulness of doing director evaluations, even in medium-sized companies. While I believe that this would be a possibility in some cases, my experience indicates that at those medium-sized companies in which shareholders are present on the board of directors, evaluating them will not always be possible or conducive. In such cases, I suggest considering something different: a company evaluation, prepared by each of the directors and delivered to all shareholders (whether or not they participate on the board of directors), the chairman of the board of directors, and the general manager.

Having a written record is a good way to prepare actions to correct the deficiencies identified, and so that the director takes the time necessary to give informed opinions as well.

While I suggest that the evaluation format be designed specifically for each company.

IV. BLIND TO WHAT IS OBVIOUS AND KNOWN

> It is not enough to be in the right place
> at the right time.
> You should also have an open mind
> at the right time.
> *Paul Erdös*

> Success is a lousy teacher.
> It seduces smart people
> into thinking they can't lose.
> *Bill Gates*

I was playing a game of chess with one of my sons, who was 11 years old at the time, when he realized that a previous move had turned out to be a bad decision, and he asked me - naively - if he could go back and redo it. Given the didactic value and the entertainment value of the game we played, I answered yes, and the results turned out positively for him since he corrected relevant errors that finally allowed him to win the game.

Now imagine for a moment that you had the opportunity to use an exclusive rule: faced with the evidence of a bad decision made at your company in the last three years, you can go back in time and, in light of the new experience gained, you can now adopt the most appropriate decisions for the future of your company. A company or organization with such a benefit (or secret weapon) would be able to reach and move along what I would like to call its "maximum potential development," or MPD. That is exactly the objective or the "mission" that those who govern companies should have: the board of directors.

In the real world, companies have the best team of collaborators possible. Well-directed, it is typically able to carry out the various tasks assigned to it. But, as possible to observe in various companies, this is not enough to ensure their success or continuity. In fact, there is a responsibility that falls on high-level management, typically the board of directors, which should, in conjunction with management, be able to anticipate and avoid the "wrong plays."

In other words, company shareholders should have a self-imposed goal of making their companies operate at maximum potential capacity. Given the difficulty involved, it is they themselves who should want to have not only the best possible team of collaborators, but also the best possible board of directors: the ultimate goal of good Corporate Governance is making sure that the company achieves the best results possible, complying with ethical and legal standards, under a prudent and controlled level of risk.

The play that Yahoo! regrets not making

Think of Yahoo! for a moment. This famous company began in 1994 at Stanford as Jerry Yang's web browser, under the name "Ulysses," later renamed Yahoo!

Co-founded by David Filo, it soon became the favorite portal for netizens, so on April 12, 1996, it opened on NASDAQ, reaching a value close to $120 billion USD in the year 2000.

But the "game" seemed to be over for Yahoo! on July 25, 2016. After a series of unsuccessful attempts to revert the company's operations, Verizon announced its acquisition of the "heart" of the business for $4.8 billion USD.

Yahoo!'s problems could be summarized as follows:

a) A chronic lack of focus, showing a permanent ambivalence between being an advertising company or a technology company, and opening space for Google to grow.

b) Slow response to the emergence of various digital media and mobile internet.

c) The worst play of all: Mr. Yang did not accept a purchase offer made by Microsoft in 2008 for $45 billion, probably out of pride and a desire to be the one to guide the company, proving that company founders may have often formed such a close bond that they cannot make the best decisions.

Lofty aspirations and the Maximum Potential Development (MPD)

The maximum potential capacity of a company is a virtual (abstract) tool that represents the "profit path" that can make the company generate the highest NPV of possible utility in the feasible lifespan if the best decisions are made, given a certain level of risk. It is therefore a function of utility, risk, and lifespan. In colloquial terms, it could be called the "golden dream" for a company.

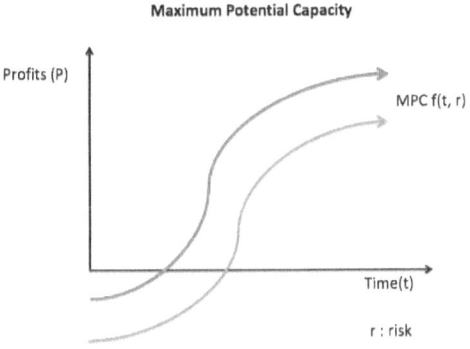

The idea is that the MPD serves everyone – but especially the owners – to set more than one goal to achieve, a way of working that reflects lofty, evolving aspirations in a way that will serve as inspiration for the changes that the company must adopt. The MPD has the gift that, unlike traditional goals, it not only involves company employees (workers) but also the owners themselves as responsible for establishing the best possible board of directors and work team to make the decisions that generate the greatest benefit for their company.

This is how the MPD can be represented graphically as a range between a maximum level (the red line) associated with the maximum utility obtained with the highest level of risk that does not cause harm, and the minimum level (the blue line) associated with the minimum level of risk that allows maximum utility to be achieved. The curves that define the indicated limits should not necessarily be parallel, and they have been represented as such just for simplicity.

The MPD can serve as a guide when it comes to preparing strategic plans since it creates an imaginary reference, but it is no substitute for a strategic plan. So why think about MPD? There are companies that successfully followed their plans for a while, even surpassing the results and paying very good bonuses as a result; but they later went into crisis essentially because the strategy implemented was only successful in the short term and was not really aligned with the MPD.

The irony regarding strategic plans and bonuses that executives are normally paid is that the true evaluation regarding their good vision and execution is in some cases obtained years later – and sometimes painfully so.

This is due to the fact that there are many ways to generate excellent short- and medium-term strategic plans that sacrifice the long-term. For example, investment in research and development (R&D) or the expense associated with after-sales service is reduced. This brings us to the convenience of incorporating the following abstract tool, the development vector.

Innovation

If a company wants to achieve its MPD, it must create mechanisms that allow it to make an asset out of innovation. Innovation does not mean that you have to re-invent the wheel. In fact, in today's world there will always be new inventions that can be adapted or used for innovation with the products or services on the market or even in adjusting business models.

Successful companies must balance use with exploration, the latter being linked to the innovation process.

In order to be successful, innovation must have a flexible structure and should, as general principles, consider the following:

- The people
- The work to be done
- Including all stakeholders
- Introducing milestones in the process that allow the hypothesis to be tested
- Coming up with multiple solutions
- Staying empathetic to the needs of potential users
- Creating prototypes and receiving feedback from users in an iterative process, from which the "obvious" errors must be learned

If you have any doubt about the importance or profitability that innovation has in your company, ask yourself the following questions:

- What risks are there of falling into the success trap?
- What are we exploring?
- At what stage are the products and services that our company puts on the market? (Emerging, growth, and maturity)

Innovation within companies can be handled in basically three ways or a combination thereof in a model that could be called "hybrid:"

- Centralized, where innovation that takes place in different business units is directed from a "center of excellence"
- De-centralized, where each business unit innovates independently
- Incubator, where a unit is created parallel to the business units in which innovation is conducted

A concept that also seems relevant to me is that of "integrated thinking,"[85] whereby, for new (innovative) solutions to be obtained, opposing ideas and limitations must be considered in order to obtain a superior solution.

Operational excellence and the Development Vector (DV)

In day to day operations of companies, a series of decisions and actions are made that mark execution and whose result is also relevant, or at least serves as part of the company's development vector.

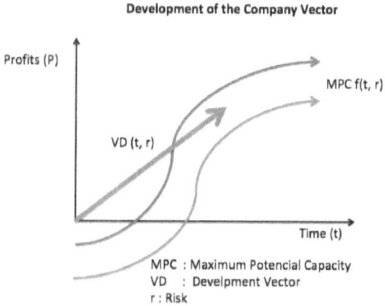

This fiction of the company's development vector (DV) must be understood, as another virtual tool responsible for positioning the company's movement or performance in relation to what, in a perfect world, should have been the decision that would have enabled reaching the "maximum potential development."

As already explained, a company's maximum potential development is related to the ability of any company, however small, to achieve the best results imaginable, assuming that it has made the best possible

---

[85] Suggested by Professor Roger Martin of the University of Toronto. https://thelearningexchange.ca/itl-project-home/itl-project-i-think/

decisions and with the only limitation being that it acts within the legal framework, complying with ethical standards and respecting the environment and communities.

The development vector aims to conceptualize the result of day-to-day actions taken in relation to the ultimate goal of achieving the company's maximum potential development.

This development vector, just like a vector would be in physics, corresponds to the result of applying the reactions that the company generates, facing the various "forces" to which it is subjected.

Some of these forces originate within the company, as is the case of the result obtained from efforts made by the fields of which each company consists: marketing & sales, production, operations, finance, acquisitions, collections, engineering, logistics, research & development, etc.

Other forces originate outside the company, such as the activities undertaken by competition, the market, regulatory bodies, interest groups, national and international economic contexts, etc.

The reaction or non-reaction to each of the indicated forces go about causing various effects within companies with cumulative results. In some cases, positive net effects (DV +) are generated with respect to what could have been the maximum potential, and in others there is an opposite or negative net effect (DV-).

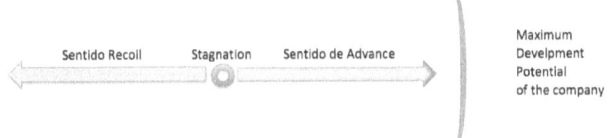

It must be noted that, according to this logic, not all internally originating forces have "positive" effects, nor do all external forces have "negative" effects. Moreover, not all the actions that generate cash have DV +, nor do all actions that generate loss have a DV-.

Here I cite some examples:

a) DVi-: If a company were to sell its products below cost due to an error in price listings, the sales area would be contributing a "negative" effect (DV-) of internal origin.

b) DVi+: If the same company were to sell some of its products below cost as part of a campaign to introduce them to the market, creating later value for the company, the marketing area could be contributing with a DV+ of internal origin.

c) DVe+: Similarly, if a competitor were to experience a problem in its logistics chain that prevented it from fulfilling orders and the company increased its sales revenue because it had the stock, the competitor would be contributing with a "positive" effect "(DV+) of external origin.

d) DVe-: Likewise, if a competitor were to experience a problem in its logistics chain that forced it to accelerate sales to avoid production loss and reduce prices, the company could see a reduced sales revenue, so the competitor would be contributing with a DV- of external origin.

Thus, as explained, the "positive development vector" as a concept will not necessarily be in tune with the company's financial results in the short term, since there could be companies obtaining good financial results that end up off the market, against the will of its owners and collaborators.

For example, it could be that the managers of a company selling rolls of photo film guessed that "traditional" photography was of an unbeatable quality and, above all, very profitable, such that they did not take the necessary measures to adapt to the demands of digital photography in time. This company could have generated large profits but "succumbed to the market years later," only because the activities that once generated a "positive development vector" (DV+) went on to generate a DV- that was in fact fatally negative.

On the other hand, an example of a widely recognized company that likely approximates the maximum potential development may be IBM. The International Business Machine (IBM) was formed in 1911 to manufacture typewriters; nowadays, it is one of the largest companies in the world. It operates in almost every country on the planet, it employs hundreds of thousands of collaborators, and its income depends on the sale of services rather than products. While it is likely that IBM has made many mistakes over the course of its history (actions with a negative "development vector" DV-), it is also a fact that the company, starting as a fairly limited business, managed to continue adapting itself to reach a very high level of worldwide activity today.

Inertia, MPD, and DV

Why might we need to consider the MPD and the DV if they are just "abstract tools?"

Think of the example of Kodak again and the feedback its executives and managers received when they looked at the balance sheet with sky-high profits in the 1990s. It was like looking at an aircraft altimeter flying 6,000 meters high but not realizing that there was a problem with the "magnificent" indicator they were seeing: it could not tell them about the 8,000-meter-high mountain range ahead.

If what happened to Kodak seems like the exception, I suggest analyzing the loss of influence that prestigious brands widely recognized at the time suffered, such as: Palm, Nokia, Blackberry, Barnes & Noble, Sharp, Polaroid, and Yahoo!, among others.

I next suggest that you recall the concept of inertia that you probably studied in school. In physical terms, inertia is defined as the inability of bodies to change the state of rest or movement they are experiencing.

Applied to business management, I recommend considering a property similar to that of a body's inertia, which explains that reaction to changes in companies is not immediate.

In other words, the difficulty that companies have developing new capacities, adapting to new requirements, adopting new configurations, creating new positions, and/or gaining access to a new market – once they have the conviction to do so – implies that there will be a delay that could prevent the company's survival.

We must add to the delay that the company's inertia presents another that in fact precedes it: the delay of the managerial staff and of those who govern the company in identifying the changes and trends occurring on the market in time and adapting the company strategy to it. This latter delay stems from several factors, only some of which I will highlight presently:

• The limitation of traditional management indicators to detect changes that will affect the long-term continuity of companies.

• The tendency of many managers to belittle the potential of actions made by competition, especially when it comes to less prestigious or well-known competitors.

• The difficulty of anticipating the enthusiasm that the introduction of new products or services can generate on the market.

• The complexity of much of the markets and industries for early anticipation or detection of the loss of competitive advantages that can push the company out of the market.

• Ignorance of customers' needs.

In summary, what I hope to do at this point is introduce the importance of developing a kind of paranoia against complacency and the dangers of inertia at the level of corporate governance, which is in turn visionary, sensitive, and flexible, and to these ends I suggest relying on the intangibility of the MPD and the DV.

Limited rationality of human beings

> Small is the number of people
> who see with their eyes
> and think with their minds.
> *Albert Einstein*

Herbert Simon (1916 - 2001), winner of the 1978 Nobel Prize in economics, stated that the rationality of the human mind is limited.[86] In very simple terms, he indicated that human beings are partially rational, that we act on the basis of emotional impulses, and that our rationality is basically limited by three factors:

- The information available
- The cognitive limitation of each individual mind
- The time available to make the decision

Daniel Kahneman, a doctor of psychology who received the 2002 Nobel Prize in economics along with Vernon Smith, proposed a model of bounded rationality to overcome the limitations of people who are supposedly perfectly rational, indicating that the brain essentially operates in two systems.

Summarizing Kahnemann's approach,[87] one could say that human thought operates under two systems. Acting under system 1 (which is rapid, instinctive, and emotional) versus acting under system 2 (which is slow, deliberate, and logical) is automatic and unconscious and aimed at protecting us from the dangers. System 2 is rational and can deal with the system 1's impressions. But the big thing is that, when

---

[86] Herbert A. Simon. Models of a Man. The MIT Press. (You may also read Administrative Behavior, a study of decision-making processes in administrative organizations, The Free Press 1997).
[87] Daniel Kahneman. *Thinking, Fast and Slow*. Penguin Books 2011.

we operate under system 2, we are not aware that we are still being influenced by – and even led to err by – system 1. [88]

Thus, Kahneman warns that system 2 does not give human beings the rationality associate with the latter (or that some believe to possess), and that the greatest deficiency can be observed in poor performance against odds and statistics, for example, unless the individual is prepared for this.

Blinded by cognitive biases

Another related element that may limit a company's ability to achieve its MPD is associated with how we make decisions. This is because human beings are subject to making bad decisions because we can create our own "subjective social reality" from the perceptions of the relationships that we have with others.

There are more than 250 known deviations[89] that affect our ability to make decisions, among which I highlight the following as examples:

- Blind Spot: the tendency to see yourself as less biased than others.

- Confirmation: the tendency to accept evidence that supports our ideas without question, being skeptical of the contrary which we consider partial or biased.

- Bandwagon Effect: the tendency to do something because many other people do it or believe it.

- Illusion of Control: the tendency to overestimate the ability to influence results that cannot be controlled.

- Gambler's Fallacy: the tendency to believe that the most probable event is the one that has gone longer without occurring.

---

[88] The terms system 1 and 2 were previously suggested by psychologists Keith Stanovic and Richard West.
[89] https://en.wikipedia.org/wiki/List_of_cognitive_biases

• Illusory Correlation: the tendency to assume that there is a relationship between variables among which there is none.

• Anchoring: the tendency to overestimate the first piece of information received.

• Availability Heuristic: the tendency to make quick decisions without having all the data, oversimplifying data that should be taken into account.

• Choice-supportive Bias: the tendency to rationalize bad decisions in order to avoid recognizing errors.

• Hindsight Bias: the tendency to reconstruct the past with current knowledge.

• Planning Fallacy: the tendency to underestimate the time needed to complete tasks.

• Confirmation Bias: the tendency to favor information that confirms assumptions themselves, regardless of whether or not the information is true.

• Negativity Bias: it is common for the negative aspect to be more attractive than the positive.

If we become aware of the weaknesses that our limited rationality is subject to, we should then look for mechanisms that allow us to make important decisions without risking the damage that they may cause.

In the case of companies, one of the recommended mechanisms is to separate the functions of company governance from administration, as long as the group dynamics of those in charge (the board of directors) are appropriate.

Patchwork solutions and time bombs

There are many possibilities for implementing measures that, even with the best intentions, go against a company's MPD, particularly when there is an incorrect perception of some variable or when the measure's effect is expected to be of short duration.

When mistaken assumptions are used, this facilitates the implementation of measures that aim to solve a problem but have the characteristics of a time bomb: that is, they have the ability to go unnoticed in the short term but can cause damage in the future. For example, when it is thought that market conditions will be ideally favorable, that current conditions will remain permanent, that customers will stay faithful, that people will behave as in a "fairy tale," when it is assumed that banks will be forgiving in difficult times, when acting in hopes that competition will not be so aggressive, etc.

In other cases, patchwork solutions – that is, temporary (short-term) solutions – are treated as though they are permanent, and these have the potential for unintended consequences that can be deactivated before they cause damage with the subsequent implementation of a definitive solution. The problem is that the final solution often does not arrive, or not in time, in which case there is an additional risk factor for the company that may end up becoming a reality.

Thus, it is not difficult to imagine what patchwork solutions could end up becoming time bombs, an internal threat that keeps the company from reaching its MPD.

The danger that may be rooted in periods of growth

A situation that should be treated with special care, and one in which a board of directors can be of enormous or invaluable help, has to do with the way that a company is managed during a period of growth and good results.

Although the previous paragraph might seem somewhat difficult to understand or even contradictory, please note that, in some companies, periods of growth have been tied to positive economic cycles that, due to their cyclical nature, end. The problem is that it is not always possible to anticipate the end of a cycle – or the appearance of a disruptive competitor or an external shock – in time, and if not, debt structures, staffing, equipment, etc. can then be excessive and result in large losses, even leading to the company going bankrupt (going from generating a DV+ to a DV-).

That is to say, positive cycles and periods of growth pose a challenge to company governance. The idea is to capitalize on opportunities in the best way possible, but without exposing the company to such risk and/or lack of flexibility that may sacrifice continuity, in case the current conditions change abruptly or at least in an unanticipated fashion.

Threats and opportunities

One of the things that happen over the lives of companies is that they are faced with both threats and opportunities. Although avoiding damage caused by the former is not always an obvious or easy task, taking advantage of opportunities is no less so, given that opportunities are not always used advantageously in moving companies along the VD+ or the "direction of advancement."

On the one hand, some of the difficulties related to avoiding the damage that threats can cause, and on the other, the proper use of the benefit that opportunities can create are because they can both have both internal and external origins, and identifying them –reacting in time – it is not always simple or obvious.

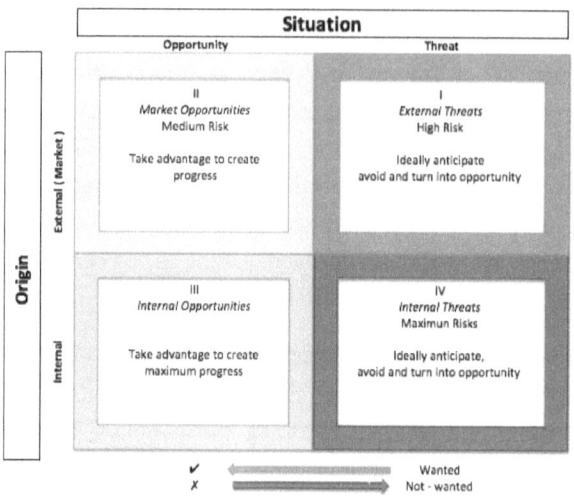

Quadrant I: Threats originating outside the business

These represent those difficulties whose origins are outside the company. Different factors, such as those related to regulatory requirements, market shocks, changes in trends, disruptive innovations, opposition organized by interest groups, etc. could be found in this category.

The ability of directors and executives to anticipate, identify, and then adequately address threats, ideally turning them into opportunities, will depend on many internal issues related to the workforce's knowledge, wisdom, and adaptability.

As in the case of Kodak, the company management's reaction did not allow it to adapt to its new settings and turn the threat into an opportunity. This was despite the fact that one of its executives, Steven Sasson, patented the first digital camera in 1975.

These types of threats are faced more effectively by companies that have a flexible culture and do not have significant inertias in the face of changes.

Kodak

A leading company worldwide with board of directors, whose internal inertia did not let it avoid the damage caused by an external threat

The "Eastman Kodak Company," better known as Kodak, started as the "Eastman Dry Plate Company" founded by inventor George Eastman and Henry Strong in 1888. Its great commercial success began with the commercialization of the paper reel– moving away from the use of glass plates used until then – and the market introduction of what was an innovative camera in those years, the Kodak 100 Vista, which used circular reels of 100 photos instead of a plate. Kodak successfully managed to make photography simple and was known by the slogan, "You press a button, we do the rest."

In 1981, Sony announced the market launch of the first digital camera that did not require film: the Mavica.

Years later, at the end of the 90s, the photography industry went into crisis when digital photography reached consumers, which quickly impacted the demand for film.

In spite of this, the "traditional" photography market reached its peak in 2000. Over the ten years that followed, it shrunk by 90%, leading Kodak to declare Chapter 11 bankruptcy on January 11, 2012.

By briefly observing some of Kodak's actions, it can be said that they reacted to the digital threat with a number of initiatives, among which I highlight the following:

1983: Colby Chandler created a division to explore new technologies such as digital images.

1986: Kodak introduced the first electronic image sensor with 1.4 million pixels.

1989: Kodak introduced dozens of products related to capturing or converting electronic images, such as scanners and printers, among others.

1993 - 2000: Kodak appointed George Fisher as CEO. He made notable changes for developing a digital strategy, but he met internal resistance from his employees since they observed that digital technology was less profitable than traditional photography.

2000: Kodak appointed Daniel Carp as CEO, who tried to bridge the worlds of traditional and digital photography.

So why did almost 30 years of Kodak's digital efforts not yield the fruits needed to gain leadership and avoid bankruptcy? While there may not be a single answer, it can at least be deduced that the traditional business was so profitable that it created an "internal inertia" that prevented Kodak from recognizing that the magnitude of the external threat that had emerged required an even more energetic, rapid, innovative direction towards the digital world.

In addition, it can be observed in Kodak's experience that the same activities related to "traditional photography" that at one moment generated a "positive development vector" (DV+) later went on to generate a DV- (a fatally negative vector, in fact) under new market conditions activated by an external threat.

Quadrant II: Opportunities originating outside the business

This quadrant represents opportunities whose origins lie outside of company management. They constitute a kind of opportunity that is not always easy to identify in time and that may therefore be tricky to take advantage of with the resources that the company has.

The benefit resulting from these opportunities is associated with what could be called "luck," as its origin does not result from the organization's efforts and may even be unexpected.

In this category, different aspects, such as those related to failures in a competitor's supply chain, greater demand for a product due to an unexpected condition (such as when a product becomes fashionable because it appears in a movie), higher demand for a service due to force majeure, etc. may be found. Opportunities that arise due to changes in market behaviors – such as demand for better or new services in an area whose population increases or as a result of changing customs or new possibilities arising from the development of new technologies, etc. – could also be considered.

The organization's overall managerial, executive, and organizational capacity to take advantage of the opportunities characteristic of this quadrant is highly relevant for the company to adapt in time and thus capitalize on the opportunity, taking actions with a DV+.

It is not irrelevant to indicate that entrepreneurial spirit and the "good nose" that characterizes many entrepreneurs is of great help in these cases.

Noteworthy examples of businesses that developed and capitalized on opportunities that originated outside the company

There are countless examples in this category, so I will mention only some of them that have been emblematic, which is why I assume they will for the most part be well known:

Microsoft: Microsoft's licensing of MS-DOS to IBM and the various developers of personal computers (PCs) satisfied the consumer need to have hardware and software at affordable prices.

Dell: The emergence of the "direct sale" of Dell Computers stirred the market for personal computers, satisfying the need to have computers configured according to the needs of each person at an affordable price.

Starbucks: Starbucks burst onto the market to sell such a widely known "commodity" as coffee, but in a way that has achieved global success. It managed to satisfy the need for a good, standardized service offered in a pleasant environment.

Tesla: In the automotive market, Tesla offers electric cars, seizing on the preference of customers willing to pay for more expensive cars and satisfying many people's interest in not contaminating the environment (or at least reducing CO_2 emissions).

Uber: The development of the app extraordinarily coordinates the demands of those who need to get around and of individuals interested in working with their vehicle, overcoming the inconveniences of conventional taxis that millions of users pointed out.

Quadrant III: Opportunities originating from within the company

These represent the opportunities that originate within the scope of the company's internal management and that are therefore expected to be used quickly and very efficiently to generate not only good financial results, but also benefits in all areas.

In this category, different elements may be found, such as those related to higher income resulting from a planned campaign or lower costs obtained as a consequence of an increase in efficiency or an improvement in engineering, etc., what I call unearthing utility reserves.

The executive and managerial capacity to unearth useful reserves, that is, taking advantage of the opportunities typical of this quadrant, can be of great relevance to the company. The actions taken in this direction can become a generative source for a relatively easy and immediate DV+.

In this category, a number of different opportunities may also be considered, such as the following:

- Developing new products and services that arise from an adequate investment policy in research, innovation, and development.

- Obtaining savings thanks to the implementation of more efficient machinery. For example, making use of high efficiency electric motors instead of normal motors and/or implementing variable-frequency drives to control pumps and fans, etc.

- Improving customer service and, therefore, sales and revenues by establishing excellent training for company personnel that is in tune with customer demands and the company's capabilities.

- Reducing accidents through training with simulators and/or improving safety levels, implementing an adequate policy that stresses and prioritizes risk prevention.

- Improving purchasing processes by not only aiming to get better prices, but to also maintain adequate stock levels, thus avoiding immobilizing items (in excess) unnecessarily.

- Etc.

Quadrant IV: Threats originating from within the company

This represents the difficulties whose origins lie within the scope of company management and are thus are often assumed to be non-existent or expected to be "contained" in time in order to minimize effects.

In my experience, the damage done to company utility due to difficulties arising from internal threats is in many cases of great importance, and it is clearly represented by the concept of what would be called an "unforced error" in some sports, as it is inflicted by members of the company itself.

What is sometimes counterintuitive is that, even when it originates within the company, it is often no less risky than the damage caused by competition from the profit angle, and it must therefore be addressed with due importance. Numerous different subjects could fit in this category, such as the following examples:

- Fines for delays caused by poor internal coordination, either with a supplier or a client.

- Customers who stop buying because they are treated poorly or because they receive a product in poor condition.

- Positioning errors in products or services, errors in production itself.

- Errors related to over-indebtedness or poor management of a company's debt structure.

- Etc.

This is a highly relevant category, but it is often undervalued since it is difficult to accept the possibility that the origin of many problems tends to be internal, so that no one can blame competition, market, politicians, regulators, etc. for the damage that these internal threats, once activated, do to the company.

For those who might not be convinced of the enormous damage that companies can inflict on themselves, I mentioned that I have seen medium-sized companies in which utility was reduced by more than 50% due to the high cost of the consequences of internal threats manifesting (not the market or competition).

Having said that, I challenge you to analyze any company you want in detail: what would have been the advantage of not having been the victim of internal threats? Can you quantify the amount of internal damages to your company?

A very particular instance of this category (IV) that deserves special attention, as it is not associated with operational issues and that in fact represents the greatest threat to the continuity of family businesses, is tied to conflicts between relatives, partners, and handling successions to the previous generation. As will be discussed later, these problems are also often underestimated.

I think it is an opportune moment to warn the reader that the way in which opportunities and threats are handled – regardless of their origin – will have significant consequences in relation to the capacity to reach the MPD (maximum potential development). If decisions are not appropriate or they are not corrected in time, if there are not high levels of knowledge, and – why not say it – if they are not received with "wisdom" in light of the "development vector," they can generate good results in the short term but incubate future damage of varying magnitudes.

Blinded by unfamiliarity with the lifecycles of organizations

To emphasize the complexity of the business world now from the point of view of the evolution of companies, and again indicating the importance of having the necessary management means, I consider it appropriate to present two models aimed at facilitating the identification of changes that companies undergo throughout their lives.

Companies, as well as people and plants, pass through different stages of growth and/or development. Unlike plants, however, if companies fail to adapt to their environment, it is not because they cannot, but because they do not want to.

The idea is not that, since the models presented below do not apply to all situations, they should not be taken as law. But I do think it is important to consider them as an element designed to stimulate awareness that the reality of companies changes over time, and that it is not always easy to adapt the organization properly and "in time."

Thinking about the life cycles of organizations can be very useful to both improving company management and avoiding the frustration of their owners.

Moreover, the models described below allow us to conclude that crises are an opportunity, and that the leadership skills that companies need over time also change. This makes it very difficult for the same person to face them adequately, especially if there is not high-level executive support.

Greiner's growth model

In August 1972, Professor Larry Greiner published an article[90] that outlined the way that companies grow, mature, and develop. According to the model, each stage of growth is accompanied by a crisis that ends it, and this gives rise to the next stage.

The model described is based on five factors: [91] the age of the company, the size of the organization (measured in number of employees and amount of sales), phases of evolution (understood as prolonged periods in which important changes do not take place in company practices), phases of revolution (periods in which significant changes occur in business practices), and finally the organization's rate of growth (the general competitive context in which it is involved).

According to my interpretation of Greiner's model, I would like to emphasize that, for him, the origin of an organization's problems is more closely linked to past decisions than to current events or conditions.

According to Professor Greiner, during their lives companies evolve over alternating stages of growth with moments of crisis whose transitions are achieved through structural changes.

---

[90] Larry E. Grainer. Evolution and Revolution as organizations grow. Harvard Business Review May-June 1998 issue.
[91] Jean Blaise Mimbang. Greiner Growth Model. 50Minutes.com.

I interpret the stages of growth, characterized by gradual changes, below:

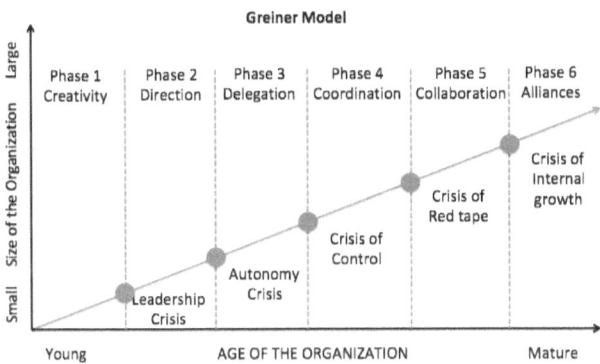

Stage 1: Creativity or entrepreneurship

This corresponds to the founding stage of the company, usually with some growing business led by entrepreneurs – not necessarily administrators – who maintain fluid, informal communication with vaguely defined positions and responsibilities, playing multiple roles with great enthusiasm.

Crisis 1: Leadership

The crisis arises when the company has grown and finds it necessary to structure the production, accounting, financial activities, etc. more formally according to the principle of specialization. The crisis is solved by hiring a manager with the necessary knowledge to implement the necessary structure. This action is not risk-free since the founders are usually tempted to interfere in activities, as they previously performed them.

Stage 2: Management

A person takes control and manages the company so that it is able to continue growing in an environment of more formal communication and with focuses in particular areas, such as marketing or finance, etc.

Crisis 2: Autonomy

There comes a time when the complexity of operations becomes very high, due to the high volume of products or services and their corresponding processes. It is then that the company can no longer be managed by a single person who tries to solve all the problems.

Stage 3: Delegation

In this stage, the company creates a structure, characterized by delegating operations from the leader or general manager to the corresponding bosses or intermediate managers, which is normally associated with the introduction of new capital.

The new executives boost the company through focused work in their respective areas.

Crisis 3: Control

At this point, the general manager who is still involved in solving the company's fundamental problems finds it difficult to leave things as they are. The problem is that the organization has grown too much to be run by a single person. The solution to this crisis is found in detailed, well-thought-out delegation, marked by the creation of departments with well-defined functions.

Stage 4: Coordination or formalization

Growth now continues with the creation of specific business units and even subsidiaries. Ideally, the company shares the same objectives, but because each area or department has its own objectives, each one enjoys a certain level of autonomy.

Crisis 4: Bureaucracy

At this point, bureaucracy has become a significant problem that has a negative effect on the organization. Growing in this way, the organization's formalities do not let the main function of the company be achieved.

Stage 5: Collaboration

To overcome the crisis, the company must acquire a new culture, aligned with the same vision, and adopt a new way of working much more collaboratively with a more flexible structure.

Crisis 5: Internal growth

Due to the collaboration stage's investment in increasing sales, lowering costs, and increasing profits, the organization refocuses its priorities. Promotions, rotating positions, and trainings allow people to maximize their work, ending in a crisis of internal growth due to "excessive collaboration."

Stage 6: Alliances

Later on – which is why many details of this last stage are unknown – Professor Greiner added this sixth stage, indicating that future growth would come from the ability to handle associations (outsourcing or subcontracting) in the functions that are not part of the basic business of the company or collaborative articulation with other entities. The advantages of this stage would be:

- Refocusing the company on its competences

- Reducing the complexity associated with the size of companies

- Containing costs

- Guaranteeing quality

- Making the company flexible enough to change suppliers and distributors, depending on its development strategy

It is important to reiterate that, for Professor Greiner, an organization's problems are essentially caused by past decisions rather than current events or characteristics of the market, considering that the historical background of an organization shapes its own future. He thinks that the future of an organization is determined by its own history, rather than by external forces.

However, it is common to see business managers more concerned about short-term results, and in some instances, they forget about basic questions like the following:

- Where has the organization been?

- Where is the organization right now?

- What do the answers to these questions mean, regarding the current direction of the company?

Complement and conflict between entrepreneurs and professional administrators

I think it is a good time to highlight a concept proposed by Chris Zook and James Allen, one that indicates that the mentality of "founders" of companies contributes to their growth and success.[92] Based on this and my experience, it seems to me that the main characteristics of successful founders could be summarized in the following points:

- Long-term vision

- Taking care of money

- Close to the "battle line," sales

- Profound ability to focus on key tasks, make quick decisions, and do so in an agile way

---

[92] Chris Zook & James Allen. The Founders Mentality, How to overcome the predictable crisis of growth. Harvard Business Review Press 2016.

- Profound ability to lead work teams, even with a range of styles (and not all of them are that of a kind teacher).

As can be expected, the ideal manager of a company will be someone who knows how to combine certain features of the professional administrator, such as order and discipline, with business characteristics, such as quick reaction to business opportunities, creativity, and the ability to inspire a sense of vision and challenge in employees.

In terms of Greiner's model, the step from stage 1 as a "new" company to 2 as an "established company" is one of the most critical steps in the life of any company.

Thus, the essence of the difficulty in moving from stage 1 to stage 2 is what could be called a "structural conflict," which often poses a threat to the existence of the organization. This conflict can be summarized as follows: the same qualities needed to establish a new business are the qualities that will then negatively affect the proper functioning of the company, sometimes fatally.

The "structural conflict" in question arises from the fact that the entrepreneur who has taken on significant personal and commercial risks to establish the business, working day and night to strengthen and promote it, at some point discovers that the business is working well, and that he can sit back, relax, and enjoy the fruits of his labor. However, the typical entrepreneur is not the kind of person who takes things easy. On the contrary, he continues to participate actively in the day-to-day activities of the company, which is growing rapidly and now requires a well-organized administration. Their participation can lead to hostility and tension, which damages the organization's ability to operate and even to survive.

For this reason, it is possible to observe in commercial organizations in Western countries numerous cases where the founding entrepreneur did not know when to ask himself, "Am I done here?", as well as many instances where this founding entrepreneur ended up ruining his own business (in English, it is known as the founder's syndrome).

Adizes's growth model

A previous comment: biological metaphors do not accurately describe the patterns of social behaviors, such as that of companies, because the latter's behavior – unlike biological organisms – is determined not only by their function but also by the beliefs, conflicts, and actions of its members. Individuals, families, society, organizations, and companies behave as complex, "dynamic systems" (that is, with many interacting parts) where the predictable, the unpredictable, the quantitative and qualitative, and chaos and chance coexist in a kind of "fabric." [93]

In 1994, Dr. Ichak Adizes proposed a model of an organizational life cycle, composed of ten stages, [94] which are in turn divided into three general phases: growth, maturity, and aging.

I present this model below, since it helps to "retain" the fact that companies are evolving and that their administration must also act accordingly. For those who wish to further study the model, there is an Adizes University (www.adizesgraduateschool.org) and several books published by this prominent author.

Dr. Adizes uses a constant analogy between the development of a person and that of an organization, as shown in the simplified diagram shown below:

---

[93] Dr. Sergio Canals. 2016. From the article, "El Cambio incesante y la estabilidad a largo plazo."
[94] To delve into the model proposed by Adizes, I suggest reading its creator in a) "Managing Corporate life cycles, how organizations grow, age and die" and b) "Pursuit for prime." Written by Ichak Kalderon Adizes, PhD.

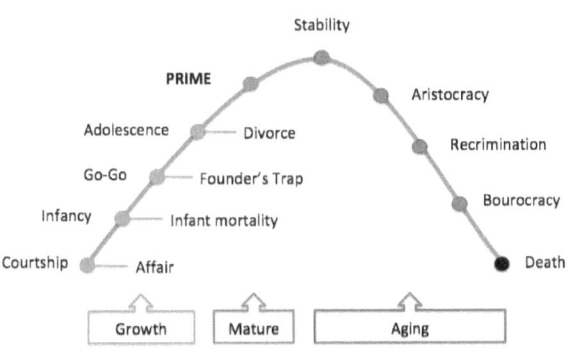

Stage I: Growth

1. Courtship or birth:

"Courtship" is the first stage of an organization's development. In this stage, the company has not been born yet. It exists as an idea in the mind of the founder(s). Courtship focuses on dreams and future possibilities.

The main objective of this stage is to build the founder's enthusiasm and commitment towards this "dream" or idea. The greater the risk, the deeper the commitment necessary.

2. Childhood:

Childhood begins at the moment when the founder takes the financial risk and leaves the paid work that he probably had, when he signs the loan papers or signs some percentage of ownership of the company over to external investors.

At this stage, organizations are necessarily oriented towards action and the opportunities that appear. The focus instantaneously changes from ideas to action. The time for talk is over; it's time to get to work and get results (sales and cash).

3. Rapid growth (go-go)

A Go-Go organization is a company that has a successful product or service, fast growth of sales, and a strong cash flow. The company is not just surviving but flourishing.

Main customers love their products or services and want more. Even investors are starting to get excited about the results.

With the success reached, everyone quickly forgets about the difficulties of childhood. Continuous success quickly transforms this confidence into arrogance.

4. Adolescence

During the adolescent stage of the organization's life cycle, the company is reborn. This second birth is an emotional moment where the company has to find a life apart from that provided by its founder(s).

This critical transition is very similar to the rebirth that a teenager experiences when becoming independent of their parents. The company "wobbles" between success and disaster.

The incorporation of a professional manager means a change in the organization's leadership; if it is not met with a change in organizational culture, it cannot support the identity of its next stage of growth.

This is a very complex stage for the founder(s), when their real interest in delegating is put to the test. It is not uncommon for tensions and divisions to appear when "the experienced founder(s)" try to adapt to the "newcomer" manager. If fights between old hands and newcomers occur normally, they will soon cease. Otherwise, there will be a divorce that may distract the organization from its focus.

Stage II: Maturity

5. Plenitude

This is the optimal position in the life cycle, where the organization finally achieves a balance between control and flexibility. Plenitude is not really a single point on the life cycle curve. It is best represented by a segment of the curve that includes both growth and aging conditions.

This is because flexibility and self-control are incompatible, so there is no stable equilibrium. Sometimes the organization at plenitude is more flexible than controllable, and sometimes it is not flexible enough.

A parenthesis to the description of the current model: if at this point in the story you feel like this model represents your reality and your company has reached a point of "plenitude" where you can feel satisfied and/or calm about the future, I suggest thinking again. Be aware that the product or service that will take away your peace of mind or leadership already exists, and that right now it is "so small" that you have not seen it... Just as happened to such notable companies as Blackberry, for example.

Stage III: Aging

6. Stability or fall

This phase, which could be called stability or the beginning of the fall, is at the top of the life cycle curve, but it is not the place to be. The most desirable position for an organization is plenitude, where the organization's vitality is at its maximum.

Companies that are in the autumn phase have begun to lose their energy, and they are aging. When an organization starts to age, the symptoms do not appear in its financial reports. In fact, just the opposite is true.

Companies in the autumn stage are often cash rich and have strong financial statements. But they are not as creative, since they think they are doing everything right. The decline begins when the entity stops being flexible, taking more and more for it to adapt to changes in the environment.

7. Aristocracy

The effects of the constant decrease in flexibility that began in plenitude begin to be more evident in the aristocratic stage. Because long-term opportunities are no longer taken advantage of, the company's focus has become increasingly short-term.

For the most part, their objectives are financially driven and low-risk. With less long-term vision, the atmosphere in an aristocratic organization is relatively stale.

In this phase, the important thing is not what is done but how it is done and who does it. Innovation and the desire to explore new alternatives – which once characterized the company – are now virtually non-existent.

8. Recriminations

When an aristocracy cannot reverse its downward spiral and the artificial repairs finally stop working, the society of mutual admiration is abruptly finished.

The aristocracy's days of palling around are over, and the witch hunt and recrimination begin.

Companies at this stage focus on who caused the problems, rather than on how to solve them.

9. Bureaucracy

Although it should be dead, the company in bureaucracy is kept alive with artificial life support. The company was born the first time in childhood, reborn in adolescence, and born again in bureaucracy with artificial continuity of its life, sometimes increasing the indebtedness based on the credibility that generated good past results.

10. Death

Death occurs when there is no one who left who is committed to the organization.

Monopolies and government agencies that are in what might be called "quarantine," due to competitive pressure and the fact that they provide an important source of employment often manage to live a long time artificially and at very high costs.

Dr. Adizes thinks that organizations go through normal and abnormal problems during each of the different stages. Overcoming them would be the key to the transition between stages, since the survival of each entity depends on them.

For Dr. Adizes, companies go about moving from one stage to another, generating two types of problems: normal and abnormal. The former occurs when a company uses resources and energy to move, successfully managing to change. The latter, when energy is used to resist, in which case it seems necessary to have external help.

Board of directors and company performance

The table that I show below has been created as a simplified tool for classifying conditions that may facilitate searching for, identifying, and focusing in on measures for action, which tend to improve the functioning of companies:

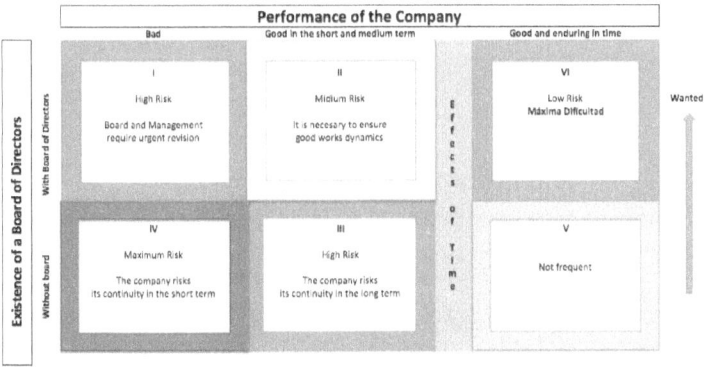

A company with a board of directors and bad results

This represents all those companies that have a formal board of directors, yet despite this, they have – whether systematically or recurrently – bad results.

In such cases, it is necessary, along with carrying out a review of the executives' powers, to do the same for the profile of the members that make up the board, the time that this body gives to its functions, and the given internal work dynamics and that which exists between the board of directors and company management.

It is important to highlight that having a board of directors does not guarantee that its functioning is adequate or that it is contributing to the betterment of the company's results. In many cases, this body is misdirected, is not adequately focused on strategic aspects, or is affected by negative dynamics (such as those explained in Chapter V).

While the a priori temptation is typically to take comfort in blaming competition for the company's problems or to believe that the source of difficulties lies in market imperfections, it is more productive to thoroughly review the internal factors that may be malfunctioning.

In this sense, as you can see in the example shown below, I will not get tired of repeating that it is vital to stop blaming external factors. On the contrary, we must focus on "freeing" all those opportunities with the potential to generate "extra utility" hidden within companies, those which only require better management to be "unearthed."

A company with a board of directors and good results

This represents those companies that are in the ideal world: they have a board of directors and get good results.

These companies face several dangers, such as letting success make the management group fall into conformity, with the company losing or not developing the necessary "adaptability."

In these cases, it is helpful to review the board's capacity to incorporate measures tending to optimize or improve results even more. Measures must also be taken to avoid incentives that favor the short and medium term, putting the long term of the company at risk. Finally, the importance of avoiding complacency, bureaucracy, and lack of adaptability should not be neglected.

The ability of the current company model to continue generating positive results in the long term should also be analyzed, or otherwise to design and implement a strategic transformation. This is where analysis of the Greiner and Adizes models can be useful, at least in understanding that the company has evolved and will continue to do so.

This may be the time for medium-sized companies to review the succession plan for founders and implement measures to avoid or manage possible family conflicts in the future.

NOKIA

A public company with a board of directors that led the mobile telephone industry until it lost its leadership.

Fredrik Idestam created Nokia as a wood pulp mill in 1865 in southern Finland. Almost 100 years later, around 1962, the company entered the world of telecommunications. During the '70s with the advent of digitalization, Nokia stood out for its ability to innovate. In 1982, Nokia produced the first mobile phone system called "Senator," and in 1984 it introduced the first mobile phone, the "Mobira Talkman." After continuous development during the 90s, it is said that, in 1998, Bill Gates himself contacted the president of Nokia to suggest the idea of developing a joint operating system to dominate the telecommunications world as he had done Windows in the world of personal computers; the project never got off the ground.

Towards the end of 2010, Nokia was in crisis despite having managed to increase revenues by 4% over the previous year and having reached sales of more than €42 billion, with profits close to €1.8 billion before taxes. [95] The share price had gone from close to $12 USD in May to $8 USD in June, and, although the company still had about 28.4% of the global market, the stock was severely punished because it lost 8 participation points in the last year, dropping from 36.4% of the market. This was due to the fact that, by the end of 2010, Apple alone, among several other manufacturers, had managed to sell more than 70 million iPhones, with their respective apps.

According to an article published by The New York Times[96] in September 2010, the suffocating bureaucracy led to a lack of action in early innovation in smartphones. The company was eaten up with its previous successes and living in a state of complacency and slowness, and was out of touch with the wants of clients. A few years before Apple introduced the iPhone in 2007, Nokia's high-level management already had on hand the prototype for a device with a large touchscreen that connected to the internet; what's more, the company had already developed the first version of what would later be the "AppStore." Engineers saw the prototype, developed by the company's research center in Finland, as a disruptive invention that would have given the largest cell phone manufacturer a powerful advantage in the cell phone market.

Therefore, it would not have been the lack of time, resources, knowledge or capacity for innovation, and development that kept Nokia from getting on the coming wave in time.

While Nokia's example leaves room for different interpretations, from at least one point of view it seems that the company did not manage to overcome a crisis of bureaucracy. From another angle, it seems that

---

[95] Nokia in 2010 Review by the Boards of Directors. http://company.nokia.com/sites/default/files/download/07-agm-nokia-in-2010-pdf.pdf
[96] Kevin J. O'Brien. Nokia's New Chief Faces Culture of Complacency. The New York Times, September 26, 2010. (http://www.nytimes.com/2010/09/27/technology/27nokia.html)

the company's management was caught by a kind of inertia of success that did not allow it to properly assess and implement the innovations that its engineers had created in a visionary way.

It seems reasonable to assume that all of Nokia's users, and especially its shareholders, would have expected that the company's management – including the board of directors – would have taken the necessary steps to maintain its leadership. Given this, some questions arise, such as the following: what role did the board play in the company's strategy? What measures could have been taken to have a board that was deeply involved in strategy and capable of leading the company to the next stage? Was the board aware of the transitory nature of competitive advantages? Was the board properly trained to detect and avoid the negative dynamics that can affect decision making?

A company with good results and no board of directors
This represents all those companies that do not have a board of directors, even though they may have had good results so far.

As explained earlier with the Greiner and Adizes models, this type of company has even more exposure to the difficulties inherent in the development of companies. They thus run the risk of not being able to articulate the measures necessary for prolonging good results.

As a shareholder, I would not feel at ease and would consider my assets to be at risk. This is where the analysis of the Greiner and Adizes models can be useful at least for understanding that the company will continue to evolve, and that good results may not go on forever.

A company with bad results and no board of directors
As explained earlier with the Greiner and Adizes models, this type of company is at an even higher risk of experiencing the difficulties inherent in the development and evolution of companies, since the

manager does not typically have someone who can help him in these "esoteric management" issues.

When these companies survive, they often do so because of the entrepreneur's push to maintain low operational costs by sacrificing the potential for growth. This type of company is not attractive to the job market and therefore runs the risk of greater deterioration in comparison to its peers.

A company with no board of directors and with good results that last over time
This represents an uncommon type of company: sooner or later they fall victim to some of the big threats made by the "effect of the passing of time" to being able to adapt in competitive strategy, innovation, the organization, or changing market requirements in order to be able to generate successive temporary comparative advantages.

A company with a board of directors and good results that last over time
This represents those companies that not only manage to get good results, but also manage to do so in a lasting way over time, as they generate successive competitive advantages in a temporary span.

Companies that can be grouped in this category are exceptional, and they gain recognition because they achieve a temporary transcendence that goes beyond the products and services that at some point could have launched them to stardom.

Companies recognized worldwide, like IBM, Siemens, ABB, and J&J, just to mention a few, could be considered as examples of this category.

HAMBERGER

Rooted in the future for 150 years

www.hamberger.de

A medium-sized company that has a board of directors and good results that last over time.

Hamberger is a family business that was founded as a match factory in Germany in 1866 by Mr. Franz Paul Hamberger.

At the time of writing this book in 2016, it has celebrated 150 years, and it has five business divisions: flooring, sawmills, toilets, shops, and forestry. The company employs almost 2,400 employees and is led by the fifth generation of the Hamberger family.

Today, they are known for "HARO" brand products. They manufacture flooring, sports flooring, and bathroom fixtures. The company exports 48% of its products to more than 90 countries, with total earnings of more than €300 million.

The company's mission statement is "We create quality of life." Its fundamental values are the following:

- Family business
- Innovation
- Dedication to customers
- Dedication to employees
- Sustainability
- Manufacturing Company
- Quality assurance
- Responsibility
- Financial success

Even though the company does not have a board of directors, it does have an advisory board that meets quarterly and is made up of five members: two who are part of the family and three who are external.

Throughout Hamberger's history, there has always been a long period of cooperation between family business leaders. This intergenerational cooperation has been one of Hamberger's most important keys for success: family cohesion and a common understanding of the company's long-term strategy have been very important. The set of rules that were established and governed over decades were written down in 2011 as what are now Hamberger's corporate principles.

For a family member to get to senior management, they must meet the following requirements:

- He or she must be able (with good education) and willing to take on the responsibilities of the position,

- and he or she must be authorized to do the job, by a vote of the general assembly.

Although the bylaws allow someone outside of the family to hold the position of general manager, this has not yet happened.

The company holds two general assemblies with the participation of all shareholders in June and December. This lets all the shareholders stay informed and vote, if necessary. In addition, regular quarterly meetings are held on the advisory board (two shareholders are members of the advisory board).

Although the advisory council does not have a formal debt limit, major investments must be approved by the general assembly.

The effect of the passing of time

From a certain perspective, one could say that the passing of time creates a kind of insurmountable abyss for a significant number of companies, manifesting as what we call "crisis." It seems inevitable that companies will face different situations that, after reaching a certain level of success, will not only expose them to a reduction their income, but to disappearing from the market. The disappearance is due to the inability to make permanent over time that competitive advantage that at some point had set it apart from it from its peers and/or made it successful. Columbia Business School professor Rita Gunther McGrath, shares something that I suggest readers explore more thoroughly, by identifying what she calls transient competitive advantages. [97]

There are many types of crises, some associated with rapid growth, others associated with lack of growth; there are also some associated with the fall and even the collapse of what was once stable income.

Each of the different types of crises requires a "special set" of actions that must be implemented at a certain time, and this is where the board – given its unique mix of strong business knowledge and day-to-day distance –has to play a role complementary to that of the executive staff in order to ensure the continuity of the company.

---

[97] Rita Gunther McGrath. Harvard Business Review Press 2013. The end of competitive advantage, how to keep your strategy moving as fast as your business.

V.   FINAL WORDS

> With audacity one can undertake anything,
> but not do everything.
> - *N. Bonaparte*
>
> The secret to life is knowing
> when enough is enough.
> - *Dr. Vincent Ryan*

We are living in an era of changes that accelerate at an ever-faster pace. Moore's Law and its effect on digital technologies, together with the consequences arising from global warming (beyond the relative differences of opinion on its origin) and globalization, have created an environment that evolves in such a way for which neither businesses nor human institutions in general were designed.

As if this were not enough, the human mind is limited by cognitive blind spots and biases that restrict our capacity for identifying the opportunities as well as the threats that come about, generating uncertainty with regards to the future.

This book has presented arguments and shown examples that at least tend to support the following:

- There would seem to be no limits on innovation: the digital age has introduced technologies that advance at a non-linear speed and that bewilder the human capacities for evaluation and administration. New technologies emerge from different areas of knowledge and intermingle to generate new innovations.

- Expert businesses are needed in digital technologies: there are still businesses that, blinded as they are by past successes, either do not manage to grasp the urgency of incorporating digital technologies or do not advance at the speed necessary for becoming digital experts.

• Company governance must master the balance between exploration and explotation: in the digital age, the risks of committing the administration errors of the past are still present, which often result more from decisions and omissions than from circumstances. Taking advantage of market circumstances in order to turn them into opportunities depends on a difficult interaction between using digital technologies and strategy; contrasting the ways in which Kodak and FujiFilm faced the same threat, typical of the digital age, is an illustrative example.

• The future is not guaranteed for even the most successful company: the rapid advance of technological innovations creates a gap with respect to traditional businesses' capacity for adaptation, which may be filled by ventures that may end up putting the position of traditional actors in their respective industries at risk.

• The risks of the past are still present: Companies that start out being led with an "entrepreneurial spirit" evolve as the years pass by, demanding change of those that are often incapable of facing it properly or with the agility needed. Companies evolve – with a certain similarity to animal life – which necessitates the development of an attitude and capacity for adaptability, in which the board of directors plays a relevant part.

• We walk in the shadow of Cognitive Blind Spots: human beings are subject to committed significant errors, given that we have limited rationality. Realizing this weakness can avoid big problems, and a well-organized board can play a role in this direction.

• Good governance is needed more than ever: currently, competitive advantages are transitory, which is why boards of directors must participate actively in the definition, updating, and monitoring of company strategy. Poorly chaired boards that do not have a proper work dynamic leave room for internal and external risks to become threats. Even when it may seem obvious, well chaired, organized boards must play a role in monitoring the continual improvement of the processes associated with the basic business of their companies.

In Chapter II, we saw different models developed by noteworthy thinkers who I am sure hope for companies to use them to be successful at present.

In Chapter III, the importance of maintaining excellence in terms of traditional governance was laid out, adding the need to incorporate mechanisms capable of facilitating quick detection of opportunities as well as threats, which advance at an ever-greater speed in the environment of the digital age.

In Chapter IV, we have gone over traditional aspects associated with good corporate governance, which, as well-known as they may be, must not be forgotten.

So the book concludes without offering a recipe for achieving success in the digital age, since that would not be believable. The only intention is for the models that have been briefly described, the limitations that have been shown, the examples mentioned, to allow, in the hands of good directors and executives: a) to develop a vigilant, almost paranoid attitude on par with the governance of companies that have the strength necessary to b) create a culture capable of asking the right questions time and again, without letting themselves be fooled by what could turn out to be a transitory success.

The opinions, experiences, and recommendations expressed in this book do not aspire to be considered a law of administration, but rather only to serve as a reference and a complement for the experience that each reader possesses and of which he will certainly make use upon finding the best way to run his business(es) or the business at which he works or advises, etc.

Finally, I would like to ask readers not to forget the following paradox: as long as you have the freedom to change, you will not feel the pressing need… which is why you must begin before it is necessary (and always keep the call for exploration alive).

I hope that this book may serve to help anyone forming a business in the digital age, shareholders, and the millions of people that work at them. Since I learn from others' experiences – in addition to my own – please do not to hesitate to send me your critiques, suggestions, experiences, and ideas at rlarenast@gmail.com.

VI. ACKNOWLEDGEMENTS

Developing this book was possible thanks to the teachings and the support of many people that I cannot name. Throughout my professional career, I have had the good fortune of working with exceptional people and having shared with very good workers, all of whom had an influence on a good part of what I have summarized in these pages with their teachings. That said, I would be remiss not to specially recognize the learning opportunities afforded me by people like Robert (Bob) L. Becker (RIP), Mike Johnston, Robert Ninker, Sergio L. Gama, Javier Fernández, Sergio Alvarado G., Eduardo Novoa, Leonardo Solari, Diego Valdés, Jorge Schwerter, Erwin Hoehmann F., and Carlos Menzel S.

I would also particularly like to thank those who made a special effort, and an entirely selfless one, for the development of this book, as did PhD Enrique Canessa, PhD(c) Victor Jara, PhD Adolfo Gutierrez, PhD Alfredo Enrione, Pablo Pinochet, Amanda Foy and Paul De Rutte.

Finally, I thank my family, for the patience that they have shown during the many months of work needed to develop this book.

www.ingramcontent.com/pod-product-compliance
Lightning Source LLC
Chambersburg PA
CBHW031631210526
45464CB00004B/1842